The Superconscious Path

Christopher Michael Duncan

Australia

DUNCAN
PUBLISHING

Christopher Michael Duncan c/- Duncan Publishing
www.christophermduncan.com

Ordering Information:
Quantity sales. Special discounts are available on quantity purchases by corporations, associations, and others. For details, contact the "Special Sales Department" at the address above.

The Superconscious Path / Christopher Michael Duncan. —1st ed.
ISBN 978-0-6458924-0-6

Contents

Preface

The philosopher's stone is an alchemical substance that's able to turn base metal into gold. It was exactly what I was looking for as I went on a journey to transform my life into something precious.

By 2018, I'd created everything I'd set out to achieve. I was married to an amazing woman, I had a multi-million-dollar business, I was in great health, and had amazing friends. Still, I couldn't shake the feeling something was missing.

I was already schooled on the idea that fixing myself wasn't needed. I understood how to connect to my superconscious and recode any limitations, yet my life felt empty, and I didn't know why.

I wasn't unhappy, so to speak. I was just...numb.

I felt like I was going through the motions of life instead of really living it. By day, I ran a successful digital marketing agency and education business from my home office on the Gold Coast in Australia. In the evenings, I would play tennis and have friends over for barbecue and drinks multiple times a week.

Is this it? I thought to myself one evening. *Do I just do this for a few more decades, and then die? There has to be more, right?*

Part of me felt guilty for even asking the question. I mean, shouldn't I be grateful and happy for what I had? My current reality was a massive shift from where I'd been just a couple of years earlier. In contrast, this was heaven. What was I missing?

I decided to find the answer, so I sat down and asked myself a series of questions:

- What would I do if I couldn't fail?
- What would I die for?
- If this was my last week, or month, or year, what would be important to me?

The answers didn't surprise me. I knew what I wanted, I'd just been hiding from it: to build a massive, world-impacting consciousness education business that would teach people all I'd learned over the past few decades.

Most of us are hiding from our truth. It takes courage to know yourself, to recognize your innermost calling, deepest fear, and most basic desire. It takes even more courage and skill to transmute all of that energy from its fearful base to the precious gift that's in each of us.

I had many doubts. My inner critic asked all sorts of disempowering questions:

- Who would listen to me? I haven't achieved enough to teach others...have I?
- Why this? Why is it so important to me? Is it worth the risk?
- Do I really want to rock the boat?
- What if I fail?

My biggest fear was failure, because I'd already experienced it. Two years earlier, I'd hit rock-bottom after the tragic death of my business partner, when I found myself in a huge financial and emotional hole we'd literally just pulled ourselves out of.

"What if I fail?" I asked myself again.

But what if I succeed?

I was in total conflict, lying awake at night planning how and what I would teach, and then by day, like an imposter, I'd forget it all and run my marketing agency. This internal conflict lasted for months. However, the idea of creating an advanced consciousness education business would not leave me, so I decided to go for it and launch the superconscious recode to the world. The mere thought of it scared the crap out of me.

Up until this point, I'd only gone for goals and results I knew others would approve of. This was an unconscious agenda based on the idea I wasn't competent. My success was designed to prove I was good enough in everyone else's eyes. Once I decided this was no longer the case, I was free to use my genius to create what mattered to me.

Launching the superconscious recode would cause me to lose friends, be called a "woo-woo," and not get invited to dinner parties and weddings. It would also be the best decision of my life that would impact millions of people, result in a bestselling book with 200,000 copies sold in its first year, and birth a twenty-million-dollar company.

Most importantly, I'd found my purpose in life.

Upon reflection, I came to realize it was the perfect decision, and I was the right person to create that business. In fact, I'd spent my whole life getting ready for it. My superconscious superpower had already been shaped and formed. By letting go of any fear and stepping into a true choice, I was able to achieve in two years what I'd been trying to accomplish for a lifetime.

I built something meaningful.

This book is about how magic happens when you use the superconscious creation process and activate your superpower.

In my first book, *You're Not Broken*, I discussed the idea that we don't need to fix or heal ourselves to be successful. In fact, by focusing on fixing or healing, we actually put more power into what we don't want.

Here, I take this idea further and share with you a clear method called the superconscious creation process. It will ensure you're in the correct structure, allowing your superconscious genius to guide you in creating miracles, manifesting your dreams, and living the superconscious path.

If you read *You're Not Broken*, you'll know my story. I was firmly rooted in the personal development mantra that I needed to fix or heal myself in order to get what I wanted. This might be your belief as well, but like many others, you've probably learned this only leads to being more stuck.

The truth is that we're a creative consciousness. We all come into this world completely open to learning and experiencing life as a human. We look to our parents and society for validation and nurturing. In the places we feel we don't get enough, we make up beliefs about how there's something we need to change about ourselves. Usually, this results in the conviction that there's something we must do, achieve, learn, fix, or heal to reclaim what we believe is lost, so we spend our life trying to create conditions and circumstances that prove us wrong. However, because the negative belief is all we know, we can never truly be rid of it.

For example, you think you're not good enough, so you go out and achieve a lot of success to prove your worth. The problem is that it will never be enough to finally rid yourself of your belief, because your unconscious (or subconscious) wants to keep everything the same.

If your unconscious has survived feeling not good enough, it will continue creating that same experience, regardless of what you've achieved. This causes a conflict in your consciousness. One part wants to finally get rid of the negative belief, and the other doesn't. Without the awareness I share in this book, you'll continue living a frustrating life, feeling like you're always chasing a dream, but never getting to your destination.

This is why the unconscious has taken a lot of heat. In fact, in some self-development circles, there's an all-out war on the unconscious. Fear, negative thoughts, and uncomfortable feelings are not allowed. It's like they believe there was some mistake in our consciousness.

This is not true.

The fact is the unconscious is doing a brilliant job of keeping us all alive. We're quite lucky to have something inside of us that doesn't want to try new things all the time. It's useful. But most of us want to do more than just survive. We want to reach our full potential, to live a life we love, and to thrive. Luckily, we've all been given a superpower to do exactly that. We just haven't been taught how to activate it.

This superpower is held in our highest aspect of consciousness, called our superconscious, which is the domain of invention, inspiration, creativity, intuition, wisdom, and genius.

In this book, you will join psychologist Michael Dunne as he learns to use the superconscious creation process of shifting from living an unconscious life to the magic of the superconscious path. My goal is that by the end, you will not only understand yourself and others better, but also know how to use the superconscious creation process with precision.

Let's get to it.

Christopher Michael Duncan
April 2023

CHAPTER ONE

STUCK

"I dread waking up in the morning. I get this sinking feeling that everything's about to go wrong. I'm barely functioning."

Mike was trying desperately to concentrate on what Cassie was saying, but he kept getting distracted by the sound of the tattoo drill next door to the right, and the *bom-chicka-wow-wow* music from the sex shop on the left.

He had a sound machine going for all it was worth, but the walls were paper thin, and it wasn't doing much to drown out the sound.

Not only was it distracting, but it was embarrassing. These people were in their weakest moments, sharing their innermost secrets with him, and he couldn't give them his undivided attention. He did the best he could to help Cassie, but he felt guilty that he probably wasn't giving his best.

At the end of the session, he walked Cassie out, because the usual suspects that loiter outside his surrounding businesses, left a lot to be desired.

Sure enough, there was a couple kissing passionately and practically dry humping in front of the sex shop. Then a guy with a greasy shirt and stringy hair came up to them and asked, "Can you spare a smoke?"

Mike hustled Cassie past the obviously drugged-out man, and he made sure she got into her car safely.

"I'm sorry about this," Mike said, even more humiliated. "I've tried talking to the landlord about it, but he says they're not doing anything wrong, so I can't break my lease."

Cassie put her hand over his. "It's okay, Dr. Dunne. You've helped me so much. That's all that matters to me."

"Thank you, Cassie. You have a good night."

As Cassie drove away, Mike looked up at his hand-painted sign that read *Dr. Michael Dunne's Psychology Clinic*, now lost behind the neon-lit advertisement for tattoos and the air-brushed photos of near-naked ladies promoting the adult store.

It seemed that "stuck" was his default position nowadays and played into all areas of his life. He was only thirty-seven years old and already felt like a complete failure.

On top of everything else. Dot, his grandmother and last surviving family member, was ill and needed specialist care. When his grandfather, Frank, passed away, his nana became his responsibility. The insurance company would only cover basic medical treatment that left her unable to think straight, and it severely affected her quality of life.

Mike had called, emailed, and petitioned the insurance company to have a heart and cover the treatment she really needed, reminding them of how many years she'd paid into her plan, but it fell on deaf ears.

This left him with a terrible choice: come up with the money himself or let his grandmother suffer with a mediocre treatment. His grandmother deserved to have the best care, but in the two years since her diagnosis, Mike had gone through his savings. Now he was out of cash.

To try and make more money, Mike had gotten his real estate license and started a second business. Based on the boom and growth of their small seaside holiday town, it had seemed like a no-brainer. With an aging population wanting to downsize and retire, he'd known Williamstown was the perfect spot.

That was before the pandemic, which frightened that age group into playing it safe. Now, the property market was overpriced, and they were in a big recession.

With two struggling businesses and increasing financial challenges, Mike wasn't spending quality time with his wife and children. The strain on those relationships was a constant reminder of just how bad he was doing. Nothing was working. He had depression and anxiety, and was taking the required medication he'd gotten from a psychiatrist friend of his.

As he usually did in times of despair, Mike took the neatly folded paper he kept in his wallet, opened it, and read aloud, "I am the creator of my reality. I attract money with ease. I am confident and courageous. Nothing stops me."

He saw this suggestion in a self-help book, but it never worked, no matter how many times he said the words. At this point, they no longer had any meaning.

He wasn't fooling anyone. This was especially true of his wife, June, who'd taken a part-time admin job to ensure the bills were paid. Even though he was grateful, he had a nagging pang of shame.

He knew that in this day and age, most families were a two-income household, but when the twins were born, they both agreed they didn't want to spend a ton of money on childcare and nannies, so June took a break from her job. At the time, it was no big deal, since he was earning enough to keep everything afloat.

But now, their carefully constructed life was falling apart. Covid had stopped the world for an entire year. Many small businesses went online or shut down completely. It was a sign of the times. Mike wondered, not for the first time, why good guys like him always got the rough end of the deal.

He needed to let off some steam, so he went to his Jiu jitsu class. He'd started going in order to relieve his tension, but it also made him feel better knowing he could defend himself against the new "clientele" that hung around his business, should the need arise.

He was going through the usual manoeuvres, when a crippling fear overtook him. He started thinking about all of his problems and how there was no way out.

"Ow!" Mike said, as he came down hard on the mat, and the hairy, sweaty knee of his Brazilian jujitsu instructor pressed firmly into his back,

"A little distracted, eh, Mike," Carlos said as Mike tapped the mat to signal he'd given up.
Carlos held out his hand and helped Mike get on his feet. "Yeah, a little. Sorry about that."

Mike bowed to Carlos and took a quick shower. As he left, he glanced in the mirror and noticed he was slouching. He'd always had excellent posture, and now it seemed he was getting old before his time. The huge bags under his brown eyes didn't help, or his unruly sandy hair, because he hadn't even taken the time to get a haircut.

Mike made his way across town to River Downs Retirement Home, the only place that provided the care his grandmother needed for her autoimmune disorder. It was also expensive and in high demand. He parked in the back, because he hadn't paid the overdue bill and wanted his visit to go unnoticed.

He could see his grandmother sitting outside her small unit in the early afternoon sun, reading a book.

"Hi, Nana. How are you?" Mike asked as soon as he was within earshot.

"Michael, I'm so pleased to see you,"

Nana was eighty-three. Before the illness and the medications, her mind had been sharp as a tack, and she was a healthy weight. But now she was much frailer, with her house dress billowing around her.

"Come inside, and I'll make you a cup of tea," she said, before getting up and giving him a big hug.

Despite all she was going through, Nana remained in good spirits. Living at River Downs meant she was able to have the independence of her own place, plus the support of the staff. It was the perfect situation for her. Mike loved that his grandmother was so looked after.

"So, how are you?" Nana asked as Mike followed her inside.

"Great," he lied. "How are you?".

There was a knock at the door, and then Gloria Hernandez, the general manager of River Downs, came in. Mike guessed her age at mid-forties. She wore red lipstick, black hair in a tight bun, and a grey business suit. She always looked put together and was a tiny dynamo.

"Hi, Dr. Dunne. I thought I saw you drive in. Can I grab you for a second before you go?" Her usual cheery expression and upbeat tone belied the message underneath, but Mike received it all the same.

He swallowed past a lump in his throat and said, "Sure."

After Gloria left, his grandmother turned to him. "How are June and the kids?"

They're doing great!" Mike replied

"It's been so long since I've seen them. You must bring them for a visit."

"I will, Nana. I promise."

After an hour of enjoying his time with his grandmother, Mike looked at his watch. It was already 2:30 p.m. and probably time to go face the music with Gloria before picking the twins up from school.

Mike took a deep breath and knocked on the door.

"Come in!" came Gloria's bubbly voice

He put on his best fake smile and opened the door.

Gloria looked up from a file she was reading. "Ah, Mike. I was just going for a coffee. Care to join me in the café?

Mike didn't really have time for coffee, but he wasn't about to upset Gloria more than she already was.

When they got to the café, she sat down across from Mike and gave her most patronizing smile. "Mike, there's no easy way to say this," she said and paused, looking like she was trying to find the right words. "You know I care about your grandmother, and I'm aware times are tough."

Mike nodded. "Yes."

Here it comes…

"Your grandmother's doing so well here, but we are running a business and have staff to compensate. I'm so sorry to say this, but if we don't have full payment by the end of the month, your grandmother won't be able to remain here. We have a long waiting list, and it's unfair to them as well. She reached over and squeezed his hand to soften the blow, but he barely felt it.

Mike once again painted on his fake smile. "Gloria, I get what you're saying, but It's not a problem. I've figured out a way to pay her bill, and you'll have the money by the end of the month."

Boy, was that a whopper of a lie. What was he going to do in eleven days when he still didn't have the money?

"Great," she replied. "I'm so happy to hear that. Well, I'd better get back to the office. Send my love to June and the kids." Then she picked up her coffee and was on her way.

Mike just sat there, head in his hands, sinking into utter hopelessness. He couldn't go on this way.

Why didn't she and Pop save more for retirement?

But he immediately felt guilty for even thinking it. What sort of man can't look after his family?

You're such a loser. He thought to himself

"You lied," a deep, croaky voice said from across the café. Mike turned around to see an elderly gentleman hunched over and leaning on a cane.

"Excuse me, sir?" Mike said, alarmed. "Were you listening in on my conversation?"

"I caught a bit of it. Mainly the part where you told her you would pay her back. But I've seen Gloria have these conversations with enough people to know what's going on, Anyway, I have a sixth sense about these things."

Mike felt the blood rush to his face as the man came over and took the seat Gloria had just vacated.

"Listen, I know your grandmother, and I was good friends with your grandfather. You need to find a way to keep her here."

"I know," Mike replied, feeling even worse. "I've been trying, but times are tough. I haven't sold a house in nearly a year. We have two children and a mortgage. It's impossible."

"Perhaps I can help,".

"Really?".

"Yes, my name is Giovani Vanderhill. You should speak to my cousin, Vance." He reached into his pocket and handed Mike a business card. "I'll call him and let him know to expect you."

What a strange old man, Mike thought. Then he looked down at the business card. It read *Vance Vanderhill*, and underneath was *Entrepreneur. Investor. Superconscious Creator.* A number was also printed at the bottom.

Superconscious Creator? What the heck was that?

Mike stared at the card in disbelief. Everyone knew the Vanderhills. They were the richest family in town. Their great-grandfather built the first hotel here when this town was only beautiful beach and a few shops. Their property portfolio was known to be in the hundreds of millions. Vance had the Midas touch, taking the already successful family name and creating a restaurant chain. By all accounts, he was a billionaire.

But could Mike really take the word of a random old man in a nursing home? Maybe he was eccentric and carried these cards around to impress people. After all, when you have them made, nobody checks if they're accurate. Mike could have cards printed that claimed he was the president.

So he just smiled and said, "Thanks."

Giovanni looked at him a moment longer and said, "I'm not some kooky old man. You'll see."

"Okay, thanks again," Mike said. "Sorry, but I need to go pick up my kids." Then he quickly excused himself, relieved to be out from under Giovanni's scrutiny.

When his business slowed down, and his hours had gotten more flexible, Mike made a deal with June that he would pick up the kids from school, which enabled her to work extra hours. He had fifteen minutes to make a twenty-five-minute drive. He wasn't going to make it, and the twins would no doubt give him hell, so he decided to pick up a couple of Cokes for them to smooth things over.

By the time Mike arrived at Williamstown Elementary, everyone was gone. Only his two kids were left standing by the gate with the principal, which was odd, as it was usually their teacher who waited with them. They were both visibly agitated.

With a smile on his face, he pulled up next to them and jokingly called out in his best dad-joke sarcastic tone, "Want a ride?"

"Dad, you're late!" Cal stated, his eleven-year-old voice breaking in frustration.

"Yeah, where have you been?" Becca said.

As the kids piled into the car, the principal walked up to Mike's window.

"Sorry I'm late," Mike said. "I'll do better tomorrow."

Ms. Murphy, a woman in her fifties with blonde hair and a kind face, wore a concerned expression. "Mr. Dunne, I'm sure you know what happened today. We're trying to deal with it as best we can. If you and your wife can make some time to speak, we'd appreciate it."

Mike had no idea what she was talking about, but he didn't want to admit it, so he just nodded and said, "Sure thing" before she walked away.

After handing each of the kids a can, Mike said, "So, what was the principal talking about? Did something happen today?"

There was no reply from either kid as they opened their Cokes and stared out the window, their brown eyes, so much like his, looking forlorn. Then he really took in their appearance. June had sent both of them off to school with neat clothes and every hair in place. Now they looked dishevelled, their auburn hair tousled. One of Bec's braids was completely undone, and Mike noticed a bruise on Cal's cheek.

"Hey, where did you get that bruise?

"Dad, don't get mad, but we got in a fight today," Bec said, a red, embarrassed glow spreading across her face. "There were boys teasing me about my buck teeth. Cal stood up for me and pushed one of them over, and then they all jumped on Cal, so I started hitting them with my backpack," she said, starting to cry.

"Wait, what? Why didn't they call us about this?"

"They tried, but they couldn't get a hold of you," Cal said. "Then they tried mom, but she was in a meeting with her phone off, and by the time she called back, it was almost time for you to pick us up anyway.

The whole mess at the retirement home had thrown Mike for a loop, and he never thought to check his phone. Now he looked, and sure enough, there was a call from the school and numerous calls from June. She wasn't going to be happy.

"We spent the afternoon in the principal's office," Cal said.

"The boys are right, my teeth are ugly, and I need braces!" Bec wailed.

Mike took this in with a mixture of sadness for his daughter, pride in his son sticking up for her, and a fear of how much braces were going to cost.

So for the umpteenth time today, he looked at his daughter's innocent face and lied to her. "I promise, we'll get you braces. No problem. And I'll talk to the school about the bullying."

"Please don't call them, Dad, it will be so embarrassing."

He didn't want to tell them he had no choice. They were upset enough already.

The rest of the ride home was silent. As they pulled into their driveway on the outskirts of Williamstown, June waved at them from the kitchen.

June was Mike's anchor. They'd been married for fifteen years, and had been through a lot together. She was aware of the pressure he was under, and yet every time she tried to talk to him about it, he shut her down. He knew it had to be hurting her, but he couldn't bring himself to put the weight he'd been carrying on her shoulders.

They walked in the door, and sure enough, June had an expression on her face he knew all too well. But then she took one look at the kids, and her exasperation was replaced with a look of horror. "Oh, my goodness. You poor babies. Are you okay?"

"Yeah, Mom, it was no big deal," Cal said.

"I need braces!" Bec exclaimed again.

"Go wash up for dinner," June said. "I'll get an ice pack for that bruise."

When the kids were out of earshot, she turned to Mike. "Where were you? I tried reaching you for hours!"

"I'm sorry. I was visiting Nana. I lost track of time."

June sighed as she raised a delicate hand to sweep her long auburn bangs off her face, a gesture that always signalled she was stressed out. "I felt so bad. My boss always makes me turn off my phone when I'm taking notes at meetings, so I'm not distracted. The meeting went over my usual work hours, so I didn't get the message, until it was too late."

Mike felt guilty for letting June down again. She'd always been so supportive, encouraging him to get into real estate, taking on the extra work, and looking out for the kids. And yet,

even though she was his partner in life, the one person he de-
pended on the most, he couldn't bring himself to share just
how hopeless he felt and how screwed he knew they were.

That night, Mike couldn't sleep, the day's challenges running through his mind. It was 2:30 in the morning, and he'd
been staring at the ceiling for hours trying to figure out how
he could make it all happen. Then he thought of Giovanni and
that dumb business card, and he laughed. It had to be a joke,
right?

"What's so funny?"

"Nothing, honey, go back to sleep I was just thinking about
something that happened today at the retirement home.

"Oh, yeah? What?"

"After I saw Nana, I had a quick meeting in the café with
Gloria about the unpaid bill." He spoke quickly, so June
wouldn't ask for more details. "Then an old guy who'd overheard us came over to talk to me. Said he was Vance
Vanderhill's cousin and insisted he could help solve our problems.".

"Vanderhill? As in, Vance Vanderhill, the billionaire?"

"That's the one. The old-timer must have lost his mind! He
gave me Vance's business card and said he would phone
ahead. You should have been there. I'm surprised he didn't say
he was related to the Pope!"

Silence.

"June? Did you not hear me? How ridiculous is that?"

Silence.

"Are you going to call him?" June responded.

"No! Of course not. If it truly is Vance Vanderhill's number,
which I doubt, he'll laugh at me! He'll think I'm a stalker, or
worse, some loser asking for a handout."

"So what? He has no idea who you are. You could pass him on the street, and he wouldn't know."

"That's not the point. First, we don't need to go begging for money, and second, I have it all figured out. I'm not making a fool of myself, because some crazy old man was looking for attention.".

June sighed. "You've been trying to fix this for months. Seriously, you're so stubborn! What's the worst that can happen?"

"It's not worth the humiliation."

"We don't have any other options, do we?"

The truth of the question stung. Despite his feigned overconfidence, he was lying when he said he had everything under control, something he'd become too good at lately.

June sat up in bed, clearly agitated by their middle-of-the-night conversation, and turned to Mike. "What if he can help us? Maybe he can give you a loan or a donation to help your grandmother. We're running out of time. What have we got to lose?"

"I'm not calling him. I don't want to be laughed at. I'll find another way."

Mike didn't need anyone else solving his problems. He was going to figure it all out.

He popped a sleeping pill and drifted off to sleep.

Two days had passed since the conversation with Giovani, and Mike was once again up in the middle of the night, worrying over his financial problems. He had nine days to get himself out of this mess, with no plan how to do it.

A month or so ago, he'd called a credit union and asked about a second mortgage. However, it came with a huge interest rate, so he disregarded this option and hadn't even told

June about it. All he needed to do was sign the paperwork. But there was a huge catch. To make the payments, Mike needed to have a small increase in business profit, which didn't seem likely. And if he couldn't make the payments, he was risking his house. It was a huge gamble.

Could he really ask her to do this?

Yes, he thought in desperation.

He'd make his pitch first thing in the morning.

"June, honey, I need to talk to you about an idea," Mike said in a calm tone while making breakfast.

June looked up from the paper. "What is it?"

"I have a way to solve the problem with Nana, I just need your support to make it happen."

"I'm listening."

"If we get a small second mortgage on the home, we can pay for Nana's care and give ourselves some breathing space to figure this out."

June had just taken a sip of coffee and looked like she was about to choke on it. "You're kidding, right?" she said, once she was able to speak.

"I've looked at this from every angle, and I can't see any other way." He gave her a pleading look, willing her to understand. "It's just for the short term, and I can pay it back, no problem." He'd been using that phrase a lot lately, but he still wasn't convincing himself.

"Michael, I'm not doing that," June said in a serious tone. "There has to be another option. I won't risk our home." She fixed him with a stare. "I will put up with a lot from you, but not your lies. You need to ring that Vanderhill fellow."

Without giving Mike time to respond, June got up and left the room.

"Okay!" Mike yelled after his wife. 'I'll make the stupid call and get laughed at. Then I expect a major apology!"

CHAPTER TWO

THE PATH OF LEAST RESISTANCE

The next morning, Mike made his way to his BMW, another thing he was stressed about, since he was behind on payments. Thinking about losing his only mode of transportation emboldened him to make the call, despite his sweaty palms and rapidly beating heart. He popped a pill for courage and dialled the number.

"Vanderhill Restaurant Group, Meera speaking," said the friendly voice.

"Ah, hello, m-my name is Mike Dunne. Can I...be put through to Vance Vanderhill, please?" Mike stammered.

"Is he expecting your call?" Meera asked.

"I'm...not sure. Someone claiming to be his cousin Giovani gave me his number and said he'd let Mr. Vanderhill know I'd be reaching out."

The voice became friendlier. "Oh, yes! Giovanni." She laughed. "Hold on, I'll see if Mr. Vanderhill is free."

What did that laugh mean? Was it, like he suspected, "Giovanni" was giving these cards out to everyone he meets? His name was probably Harold, and he liked playing practical jokes.

As the seconds ticked by, Mike came closer and closer to hanging up. He didn't need to do this. It was emasculating and desperate.

He had his finger poised over the "end call" button, when a male voice said, "Mike, are you still there? Sorry to keep you waiting, I was in the middle of a board meeting. I'm so glad you called,"

"You are?" Mike asked, a little surprised.

"Yes, in fact, as soon as Giovani told me about a chance to help out old Dunny's grandson, I've been eager to hear from you."

"Wait, you knew Pop?" Mike asked.

"Of course. He used to work around our house, painting and doing maintenance when I was a child. He taught me to fish, among many other things."

Wow, Mike thought. *What are the chances?* Vance must be in his late sixties, so Pop would have been twenty years his elder. Still, it made sense they would have crossed paths in this small town.

"I hear your grandmother is unwell, and you're in a tight situation. I would love to help. How about you come meet me tomorrow at Fritz Point, and let's figure this out together, okay? How's ten a.m.?"

Mike was stunned and tongue-tied, but he managed to eke out a "Sounds great."

"Excellent. I'll meet you in the parking lot by the kid's playground" He paused for a moment, and then said, "Don't worry. It's all going to work out," before abruptly hanging up.

And there it was. Quick as a flash, the call was over, and he was staring at his phone in disbelief.

Mike replayed the conversation a couple of times. Then he called June to give her the news.

"I'm so proud of you for calling him," she said, in a tone Mike hadn't heard in a while.

"Thanks." Mike paused, thinking about Vance's final words. "He said it's all going to work out. What did he mean by that?" Mike asked.

"I can't wait to find out," June said with excitement.

"Same," Mike replied, with less excitement.

At nine a.m. the following morning, Mike made his way to Fritz Point, an amazingly beautiful beach with white sands and clear water. It was voted top twenty in the world and was the main draw for the tourist town. It was, however, a strange place for a business meeting.

Mike arrived early and saw a beautiful black Rolls Royce glistening in the sun, already parked and waiting. It had to be Vance. Mike parked his car and made his way over.

An older gentleman, nearly six feet tall, jumped out of the Rolls and made his way over to Mike with his greying hair flapping in the wind, a pregnant pot belly protruding out proudly, and a dark tan that would make anyone jealous. Mike could see a Rolex on his left wrist and a handful of expensive rings sitting proudly across his fingers. He was the exact image one would expect of a billionaire, and Mike couldn't help but judge him.

What's he compensating for? Mike thought to himself.

Mike chose to ignore his pang of fear and anxiety and did his best to walk with confidence, while trying to convince himself he didn't need to pop a pill.

Vance met Mike with a beaming smile and a huge bear hug.

"You must be the famous Mike Dunne. It's so great to meet you! Let's walk," Vance said. As they strolled along the boardwalk, Vance didn't wait to dive right into the conversation. "So, Mike, tell me what's going on."

It took about twenty minutes to share the full story.

He started from the beginning, about how he'd lost his parents in a car crash when he was seven, and his grandparents raised him, even paying his way through college. He talked about how heartbroken he'd been when his grandfather died two years ago, and that his last wish was for Mike to look after his dear Dot.

"At the time, I was working a government job, so I figured it was time for me to take a chance and start my own practice." He sighed. "I was doing well, and then Nana was stricken with an autoimmune disease. I thought starting my real estate business would keep me afloat, but then the pandemic hit, and well..."

It felt good to share the whole story. It really was a huge problem, and he'd done nothing to deserve all this. It was especially good knowing the person listening could solve all of his problems with the stroke of a pen.

Vance took it all in, not saying a word for what seemed like an eternity. Finally, he broke the silence, "Well, that sounds like an awful lot to take on, Mike."

Mike nodded. "It's been a heavy burden."

"Can I be blunt with you?" Vance asked.

"Yeah, sure," Mike replied.

"You really are a master at creating situations where you're helpless and need others to save you."

"Excuse me? You're joking, right? I didn't create any of this!"

"I'm sorry, but I'm going to have to disagree. Even you would have to admit that all of your problems have a common theme."

"Yes, but…"

"Look, I'm happy to help you, but it's going to take you making some changes."

Mike was stunned. He was a trained psychologist with a master's degree. He didn't need a lecture from a silver-spoon-fed billionaire heir. But he did need money, and Vance had lots of it, so he decided to humour the old buck.

"Okay," he said. "I'm willing to hear you out."

"The reason I've been so successful is because I have an understanding of the Universe that most don't."

"I see," Mike said. Typical billionaire, thinking he knows everything. It's so easy for people with all the money.

"I don't think you do." Vance replied.

Could the man read minds?

"Did you know that energy always takes the path of least resistance?"

"Sure," Mike said, puzzled by the question

"You're probably wondering why I'm telling you this. Let me show you," he said, while taking off his shoes and then motioning for Mike to follow him onto the sand.

It was a warm summer morning. Mike took off his shoes and stepped onto the sand. Just the feel of it beneath his bare feet made him feel calmer and more grounded. It had been years since he'd come to the beach. He and June used to make the trip all the time when the kids were young. Mike decided that once he solved his problems, he would bring her here. The thought of them having a fun, carefree day brought a smile to his face.

Vance interrupted his daydream. "Look at this water; it's following the law," he said, pointing to a small, thin stream of water making its way down to the sea. "Can you see it's flowing downhill, assisted by gravity?"

"Yeeeaaah," Mike said, still wondering where this was going.

"If I take a rock and place it in the way, the water will go around it. And if I dig a deeper path, the water flow down it instead. It has no choice. It flows along the path of least resistance. This is a law,"

"I get all that, but what does this have to do with my situation?"

"As humans, we also live inside this law. We're a conscious energy source, moving through time from one point to another. The results we produce, the actions we take, and the circumstances and conditions we experience, are along the least-resistant path." After this rousing speech, Vance seemed quite impressed with himself.

Mike was less impressed. This sounded like a lot of "woo-woo" talk. "Yes, it does make sense. I understand how water flows, I'm not an idiot. But again, what does this have to do with me??"

"You're like the water, flowing toward financial ruin, needing help from others. It's why you called me, right?"

Mike nodded grudgingly, too frustrated to speak.

"I would also guess that you didn't really want to, but you had no other option."

Okay, so maybe the man was more perceptive than he thought.

"My wife made me."

Vance chuckled. "That's what I thought." Adding to the truth bomb, Vance took the bitter facts a step further. "You seem like a proud man, and you're no dummy, so you've probably spent months looking for a way to solve your problems, not wanting to ask for help. I assume you're at the point where it's either me or the bank?"

"That about sums it up. I'm at the end of my rope."

"I hear where you're coming from. This is how most people come into my life, before I initiate them into the magic of being a superconscious creator."

"I saw something like that on your business card. What does that even mean?"

"It's about restructuring your life, so you can flow in alignment with your true nature, activate your highest intelligence, and use the natural laws of creation to bring your desires into reality. You see, most of us are born into the wrong life focus, so we constantly end up creating what we don't want and getting frustrated about it. You would understand this, being a psychologist, right?"

"I'm not quite sure what you're getting at."

"Most people aren't living a life they love, and as a result are unsatisfied with their reality."

"You were born a billionaire. What would you know about regular people trying to get by?" Mike said, with a note of bitterness in his voice. "Life is a struggle for most of us"

"It can be," Vance agreed. "I've had my struggles as well. What I don't tend to share with the world is that my life was far from easy. Yes, my grandfather was a big success. However, my father had a very different experience, and as a result, my childhood was no fairy tale. Since I know a lot about you, let me share with you a little about my life. I think it would help."

Mike was definitely interested in hearing Vance's story, having only picked up what he could from the tabloids.

"Being the son of a successful man put a lot of pressure on my father. Because he never had to work for anything, he had no purpose, no meaning, so he squandered his trust fund on drugs, alcohol, and good times. As a result, he was cut off from the rest of the family, so by the time I was born, we had nothing."

Mike was blown away by this information. It was the exact opposite of what he'd imagined.

"Do you know what it's like living with an alcoholic drug addict father? It's a war zone. I grew up too fast, protecting my mom and two sisters from his violent temper. I learned vulnerability was weakness, and I should never display it. Then when I was thirteen, my mother finally had enough and ran away, taking my two sisters with her, and I never saw her again. I was so angry at her for leaving me alone with him."

Mike thought back to his own childhood. Even though he lost his parents when he was young, at least he had two loving grandparents who took care of him.

"By the time I was fifteen, I'd heard many stories about who my grandfather was from my father's perspective, and from all accounts, he was a cutthroat, ruthless, and mean businessman, bent on success. I wanted none of the wealth, and I definitely didn't want to be like my father. So as soon as I could, I packed up all my things and joined the army, where once again vulnerability was the enemy, and strength was rewarded, so I fit right in."

Mike just stood there, shocked. He couldn't believe this successful man, who everyone assumed had it easy, lived such a hard life.

"Fortunately, I never made it to combat, because of an accident in a training drill. I broke my pelvis and both my legs. A week later, lying in the hospital, I got the news my father had died. I was now unable to walk and completely alone."

"I know how I felt when my parents were taken from me. I can't imagine what I would have done if my grandparents hadn't been there."

"Yes, well, sometimes good things happen when you're at your lowest point. The death of my father, the injury, and my slow, agonizing rehabilitation, forced me to confront my biggest fear; that I might actually be weak and vulnerable. And this is when I got an unexpected visit from my grandfather. Like you, I thought he might feel sorry for me and hand me a check to solve my problems. Instead, he took one look at me, feeling sorry for myself, and gave me the same offer I'm giving to you. He told me the secret to his success was walking the superconscious path and that there was a process to consciously creating anything I desired, which he was willing to teach me if I wanted." Vance said chuckling to himself.

"What?"

"I'm just remembering how crazy I thought he was. 'Superconscious path?' But I figured maybe if I played along, the old man might help me out, so I did."

Mike looked down, embarrassed. It's exactly what he'd just been thinking a few minutes ago.

"Anyway, I met the other side of my family, including Giovani, and was shocked to see they not only had financial wealth, but they were also happy and healthy. It was quite different from the picture my father had painted, so I decided I would take my grandfather's offer and learn from him."

"I assume you made the right choice."

Vance nodded. "I did. He told me that if I listened to him, I would unlock my ability to manifest and create what my heart desired. The first thing he taught me is what you're starting to understand. It's okay to be vulnerable and accept help. He also explained that part of activating the magic was to pass it on and teach it to those who are open, willing, and courageous enough to follow the path. Even though it was the hardest thing I'd ever done, I decided I didn't have much choice in the matter, since I literally couldn't walk. This is how I found my superconscious superpower."

"Superpower? What are you, an Avenger?"

Vance smiled. "Better. I don't have to wear a cape and fight crime." Then he got serious again and said, "So, after rehab, I was nineteen with nothing to my name. My grandfather sat with me daily, teaching me everything he did to become successful. I listened intently and soaked up his knowledge."

This was making Mike miss his grandfather even more. He used to have long talks with the man, especially near the end.

"I'd received a discharge payment from the military, so I used it to purchase a little steak restaurant." He shook his head. "I was so naïve. I had no experience. All I knew was that I liked steak. But over the next thirty-five years, we took our little restaurant and expanded it to the global company it is now, that employs tens of thousands of people."

"Wow. And here I was thinking you made your success on the backs of others."

"Mike, I never got a penny from my grandfather, but I received so much more. He gave me knowledge, which became wisdom to put me on the right path, unlock my superpower, and create magical results."

Mike nodded. "I can only look at the results to know you're right."

"I also reconnected with my sisters, who are now both successful in the truest sense of the word, and I went on to create many successes that have nothing to do with wealth. I met my wife and started an amazing family. We opened a charity that helps veterans rehabilitate to civilian life, and I've mentored hundreds in the creative orientation, so they could achieve their own success. There was no silver spoon, only the willingness to listen and a lot of hard work."

Mike shook his head. "I'm sorry for what I said earlier."

"No worries. I can see how you'd draw the wrong conclusion. But now that you've heard my story, I hope you know that with the right education and mentoring, you can shift your life from the unconscious path of frustration, self-sabotage, and dysfunction, to the superconscious path of a life you love." He took a hard look at Mike. "I know you're a smart man with multiple degrees, but are you happy?"

"No, not really," Mike replied. "I'm not."

Vance nodded. "Most people aren't. But if you'd like, I can teach you what my grandfather taught me. It's shaped at least two happy, healthy, heart-centred billionaires that I know of," Vance said and smiled.

"That sounds good to me," Mike said.

"Great. Let's start with structure. The water flows the way it does because of the structure it's in. If you want the water to flow to a different place, you need to change its structure."

"Are you saying humans are the same way?"

"Correct. You also flow to a predictable result, and it's because of the structure you're in. We need to shift your structure, so you can flow easily to what you want to create, instead of living in a repeating pattern of avoiding pain, like you have been."

"What do you mean by that?"

Structure is the most important secret in regard to manifesting, because it dictates how something moves. The structure the water is in is made up of sand and rocks. If we rearrange them, the water flows differently, right?"

Mike nodded. "Yeah, okay."

"So, when it comes to creating our life, we have a choice. We can live in the creative structure or the problem structure. The creative structure is made up of your current reality and what you would like to create. The problem structure consists of your current reality and an unconscious wound. I can tell which structure you're in, based on what you've already told me."

"Really?"

"Yes. Unfortunately, you're living in the problem structure. This is what causes you to constantly end up feeling helpless and needing to be saved financially. It's also why, no matter what you do to fix yourself or heal, you can't seem to change your results. This is because the structure needs to change, not you. Your structure began when your parents died, which was an unimaginably horrible experience, and it created an unconscious wound. You felt helpless, upset, and vulnerable. Your unconscious mind learned that you were powerless to change this reality, and that everything you love will be taken from you, so you created a strategy to avoid feeling it again. You made sure to keep your family together and avoid being rejected by only relying on yourself."

"This is a lot to take in," Mike said.

"When my grandfather first introduced this concept, I felt overwhelmed, as well, so let me break it down. The problem with this method is that in order to not feel this wound, you must always carry the fear or worry of that pain with you. This means you'll always find a way to experience a small part of it, and then use the same strategy to escape it, so it becomes a life pattern."

"Are you saying that my shutting June out was me trying to keep us together?"

"Right. Most people are stuck in an unconscious life-creation structure, with no conscious knowledge of why they can't change their results. They think there's something wrong with them, so they try a new strategy, or attempt to fix themselves, not realizing that by taking this approach, they reinforce the structure and get more of the same, when what they need to do is create a new structure."

Mike laughed. "All I've been thinking lately is about how stuck I am and how there's no way out of it."

"Exactly! This is totally normal and is exactly why so many people can never create the body they desire. Or they bounce from marriage to marriage, always feeling lonely and searching for love. Or a new illness keeps popping up after they finish curing the last one. Its even why people struggle to create wealth and are always dissatisfied or unhappy, no matter what they do. Without changing their structure, they always end up producing the same result. It's totally predictable. Just like the water will always flow down the same path."

"If I understand what you're saying, all I have to do is change my structure, and I'll change my results. To use the water analogy, if I dig a different path, my life will flow to a different end point."

"That's precisely what I'm saying." Then he looked at Mike and said, "About thirty years ago, my grandfather taught me the laws of superconscious creation, which have been passed down for thousands of years and are the secret to our family's success. I will happily teach them to you, if you're courageous enough to learn."

"This all sounds wonderful," Mike said. "But I don't know if I have that courage within me. I think at one time I might have, but now I feel so weighed down."

"Well, it's your choice. It won't be easy, but it will be the most important thing you ever do."

Mike turned to gaze out at the ocean, deep in thought. "I don't know..."

"I guarantee that once you learn and apply these laws, you will meet all your obligations and create so much more. Your life will be magical!"

Hope, confusion, and scepticism went through Mike in quick succession as he stared at Vance, trying to figure out if he was just a crazy, rich billionaire, or if he could truly deliver on his promises.

After a few moments, Vance took a deep breath and said, "Or, if you'd prefer, you can take a much easier path and stay in the same structure. I'll write you a check to solve your current problem, I think fifty thousand will cover it... in honour of your grandfather." He reached for his check book and started filling out a blank check right on the spot.

"What? Fifty thousand? You're joking!" Mike exclaimed, quickly brought back to reality.

"Not joking," Vance said without looking up.

Mike's mind reeled. This is exactly what he'd been hoping for. But then his brain caught up with Vance's words. "Wait, did you say I could have the training or the money?"

"That's right.".

"Can't I have both?" Mike joked as he looked at the billionaire tycoon holding the answer to all his problems, as usual, his humour covering up his nervous tension.

Vance laughed. "It's not that easy. It's like being pregnant. You either are or you're not. There's no in between. If you're going to live the superconscious path, you must let go of the old structure. You can't be both a powerful creator and a powerless victim. You can either stay in the same structure, yet again getting saved, or you can take your power back, receive the education you need, and create a new and amazing life, being rich enough to pay for anything you desire. It's your choice."

Mike's need to be saved waged war with his longing to have everything Vance promised. "The thing is," Mike said, "if this was just about me, the decision might be easier. But I really don't want to gamble with my grandmother's health. I only have about a week to come up with the money for her continued care."

Vance studied him. "I understand it's a tough decision, but I can only teach someone who's all in on learning to use their superconscious to create what they want. With the correct understanding and training, there's no gambling involved with your results. By the end, you'll no doubt have what you want."

This all sounded great, but despite what Vance said, he'd be putting everything on the line. They could lose the house...his car. Not to mention his grandmother's health. He was still running two struggling businesses. And if he turns down the money, June will be furious when she finds out.

So he stood there, on the brink, one foot in the promise of a new life, the other in the safe zone. On the one hand, he could walk away with a check, no questions asked. On the other, Vance's promise of the life of his dreams, was tantalizing. If what he said is true, then Mike's current situation could take a miraculous turn.

Vance sighed. "I can see you're struggling with your decision, so let me ask you this. If you take the money, what happens next year?"

"I don't know."

"Well, I'll tell you. You'll be right back in the same place you are now." He sighed. "Mike, I've only known you for about an hour, but what's obvious to me is that if you only wanted to be saved, you wouldn't have struggled so hard to call me in the first place. There's nothing wrong with being saved. It's just not what you want"

Mike put his hand to his forehead. "All I know is that I can't go on like this. And you're right. If I accept that check, in a few months, I'll be scrambling to find a way out of another mess."

"Well, there's your answer, man!" Vance exclaimed. "What you really want is obvious."

Mike laughed, "It's true," he said. "But, Vance, you do realize this is what I've been doing. Trying to get it done without being saved. It hasn't worked."

"Yes, it may seem like that, but I think your actions tell a different story. It's why you're so stressed, and also why you started the real estate business. You've actually been guided by your wounded beliefs. You fear that if you let people down, they'll abandon you. I think you're so caught up in the unconscious wound, all you see are solutions to get some relief from the anxiety of it."

Mike gulped. The truth hurt a little, but Vance was right.

"Anyway, there's lots of learning to do, if you choose it. You can have the money, or you can have me as your mentor and gain the knowledge, but you can't have both. So, are you all-in?"

Mike knew it was the opportunity of a lifetime to learn from a self-made billionaire who was everything Mike wanted to be.

But how could he give up a guaranteed $50,000 get-out-of-jail-free check?

He was caught between his head and his heart, but he knew what he had to do.

"I'll take the money," Mike said, holding out his hand with a grin."

Vance laughed.

Mike laughed with him as he pulled his hand away. "Okay, Vance. As scary as it sounds, I'm all in."

"Let's do it!" Vance said, shaking to confirm the deal.

Mike felt he was doing the right thing, but there was still a nagging voice in the back of his mind, screaming that he was a fool, and the money would solve everything. Only time would tell if he'd made the right decision.

Vance pulled a notebook from his pocket and handed it to Mike, along with a pen.

"Mike, write down the first principles," Vance instructed. They are as follows:

Energy takes the path of least resistance.

It takes courage.

You must be all in."

Mike did as he was instructed. He felt excited, this was the beginning of his new life.

CHAPTER THREE

THE THREE STRUCTURES

Mike was excited to begin the process. His whole life, he'd been searching for answers to the human experience. It's why he became a psychologist and attended countless seminars. Now here he was, getting his instruction straight from someone who'd achieved everything he'd ever dreamed of.

"Mike, if I asked you what makes someone successful, what would you say?" Vance asked, as they walked along the beach.

"Hmmm, that's a tough one. My whole life, I've measured success by what I've achieved, like my degree and starting my practice, and how accomplishing these goals made me feel."

"Okay, and what do you think is the strategy most people use to create success?".

"Every successful person I know has an amazing attitude. They're real go-getters. They receive a good education that leads to an amazing job. Then they get married to someone they love and fill their life with fun and joy."

Vance nodded. "There are tons of books that rave about the most efficient way to create success, and they all say pretty much the same thing you did about having a positive attitude that propels them to greatness. But from my personal experience, most fall well short of giving you a full system to achieve results predictably. The most efficient way of manifesting what you want out of life is the superconscious creative process, yet many would have you believe there's something you must do to fix or heal or improve yourself before you can be successful."

"Yeah." Mike laughed. "That's what keeps me in business,"

"Well, I'm sorry to tell you, but the creative process isn't about therapy, or self-development, or positive thinking. It's also not about self-esteem, hustling, hard work, overcoming barriers, natural talent, or tricking the Universe with some weird technique, but when you apply it and create what you want in life, it can look a lot like these things.

"Okay, now you've lost me," Mike said.

"Let me put it a different way. The result of the creative process is to successfully produce what you desire. Because you've created this successful life, you're positive and happy, it looks like you've solved all your problems. You have unlimited energy, motivation, and enthusiasm. I mean, it's pretty easy to feel great when you have everything you've always wanted."

"Right," Mike said, nodding.

"So, this is where many get it wrong. They look at those who've achieved success and determine their current attitude is what caused it in the first place, instead of realizing the person is this way, because they know exactly how to create what they want." Vance chuckled. "They have it all wrong. They've put the cart before the horse."

"Wait," Mike said. "Are you telling me an awful person with a crappy attitude can achieve success in the same way an upbeat, driven person can?"

"Yes! Most self-help gurus would have you believe that focusing on healing, positive thinking, and all the rest, is the cause of success, yet this flies in the face of many successful people who aren't positive, didn't work hard, and were able to reach their goals in spite of obvious personality flaws."

"That's crazy."

"Now, listen, I'm not saying there's anything wrong with being positive or healing yourself. I'm just explaining there's no specific way any of us needs to be in order to become successful. In fact, the focus on becoming a different person actually keeps the problem alive for longer. The reality is, you can create whatever you like and be exactly who you are. You're not broken. You just need to learn how to live in a new structure."

"So, I've been looking for solutions while remaining in my same structure, and that's why I'm not getting anywhere?"

Vance nodded. Right. There's only one constant in all success stories, and that's the structure a person is in. There isn't one religion, diet, or mindset that works for everyone. Some are positive, some aren't. Some work hard, some don't. Some get up early, some sleep in. This is because the structure of something influences the available action, which determines the result. You can put a different person in the same structure and get the same result, while putting them into another structure will achieve a different result. The structure determines the outcome, because energy will always take the path of least resistance. Our consciousness is a form of energy, so the structure in which you place the energy is what guides you. Like the water example I gave earlier.

"Okay, I think I understand the concept, but I'm still unclear about the word 'structure' the way you're using it."

"A structure is anything that has two or more parts working together," Vance replied. "There are many types of structures, and they're held together by tension. Whenever there's a discrepancy in tension, there's movement."

"So, with your water example and how it flows downhill, is gravity creating the discrepancy?"

"Yes. When there's a difference in tension between two points within a structure, a movement occurs to bring it back to equilibrium. You might have heard of the law of attraction, but a more accurate term to describe this phenomenon is the law of *tension*. So, while it may seem like the water is *attracted* to going downhill, or someone is *attracted* to money or struggle, the truth is that the energy is following the law, in that it takes the path of least resistance. To put it another way, if we wanted the water to flow in a different direction, no one is silly enough to tell the water it needs to be different, wake up earlier, or heal old wounds. We'd just dig a different path or remove some obstacles, right?"

"Okay. But how does this pertain to my current situation?"

"Because you are in the wrong structure!"

Mike blew out a breath. "This is so much to take in. I find it hard to believe that putting me in a different structure would somehow magically change my life."

"I understand where you're coming from. Let me make this more concrete for you." Vance pointed to a dad pushing his young son on a swing. "The swing is in what's called an oscillating structure. As you put energy into it, the swing moves forward only so far, before it comes hurtling back the other way. Most people live like this. It doesn't matter how much energy they expend, they move forward for a little while, and then back, eventually ending up in the same place. Sound familiar?"

"A little too familiar. It's the pattern of my life, not to mention the diets June always puts me on, where I immediately gain back the weight."

Vance Smiled. "Can you see how pointless it would be to get annoyed at the child for always coming back after being pushed? Or for the child to be upset with himself? No matter how much positive thinking either of them engaged in, the result would be the same."

Mike shook his head and laughed. "You're right."

They walked over to watch the children playing. Shrieks and laughter filled the air, the sound of pure joy that would make anyone smile. The two men leaned on the safety fence to watch them, soaked in the pure happiness only young kids at play would allow themselves to have.

"They can teach us a lot," Mike said, motioning to the kids.

"Sure can," Vance replied. "Most adults have lost the ability to just enjoy life, haven't they?"

"Yeah. I see my own kids playing make believe, and I sometimes wish I could go back to a time when I was that carefree."

"It happens to all of us. At an early age, we're taught that we must earn the right to get what we want. And as we get older, we continue to judge ourselves against others, believing we need to try even harder, striving for some perfect ideal. Failure isn't an option, and you can never lose control. If we're unhappy, there must be something wrong with us. Our childish love of play is looked down upon, so we leave it behind, believing it's somehow a negative trait." He turned to Mike. "What would your life be like if you were only playing a game?" Vance asked.

Mike shrugged. "I have no idea."

"Well, go ahead and imagine how it would feel if everything you wanted to create was a fun game played with a group of friends."

Mike closed his eyes for a moment and thought about it. Just him with his friends and family, playing in the sand with a beach ball, laughing and carefree. "It would feel great. It's a pity life isn't like that."

"Yes," Vance agreed. "It's a real pity. And we'll return to this concept, but right now I want to teach you about the stuck structure. For instance, take this fence." He said while pushing against it. "No matter how much energy I exert, the fence won't budge, because a stuck structure won't move, unless you break it. Some people's lives are like this."

"I get it, don't break the fence," Mike said, laughing. "No, but seriously, I see this with my patients."

At this point, a children's soccer ball rolled over, a misfire from a game being played about fifty feet away.

"Ah, magic!" exclaimed Vance, as he wound up a kick and sent the ball flying over to the children. "The ball is in the third structure, known as the flowing structure. When you put energy into a flowing structure, it moves in the same direction, until it rests at the end result. This is the best structure for you to be in with what you want to create."

Mike drew the three structures in his notebook.

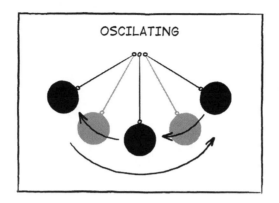

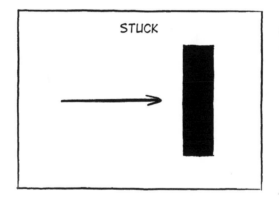

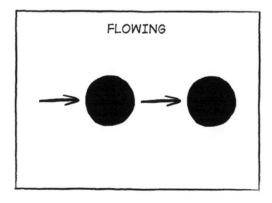

He looked at his scribbles. Did he really give up $50,000 for this?

"Vance, I appreciate the science lesson, but how is any of this going to help me make the money I need?"

"Okay, I'll put it as simply as I can. When we're not getting what we want out of life, it's because of the structure we're in. Once you shift the structure, you flow easily toward success."

CHAPTER FOUR

FOCUS CREATES STRUCTURE

They went and picked up their shoes before walking over to a park bench to get some shade.

"One of the first lessons my grandfather explained to me was how we create our structure. He said that all of us are faced with an internal conflict, because different parts of our consciousness want different things. There's the self-conscious-thinking part of our mind. It wants quality. The good life. It strives for things to be different or better. It's critical and logical, so it believes some things are good and others are bad. The self-conscious wants you to be rich, have a great body, live on purpose, go on vacation to exotic places, get praise and acknowledgment from others, and all the other good stuff we write down at a goal-setting workshop."

Mike laughed. "Yep. Some of the books I've read have instructed me to do just that. I even carry a paper around that reminds me about how I attract money with ease and that nothing can stop me. It's never worked, yet I keep trying."

"Don't feel too bad, Mike. You're not alone. But I'd toss that paper if I were you," he said with a grin. "Now I'd like to talk about the second part of our consciousness, the superconscious. It's a traditional term for an aspect of our consciousness that seems to exist above and beyond the limitations normally assumed by the self-conscious mind. The superconscious has been called by many other names, such as the higher self, the inner teacher, creative inspiration, and the voice within."

"Yeah, I've heard those terms before."

"I'm sure you have. The superconscious holds our genius inspiration and intuition. Now, the third part of our consciousness is the unconscious, which is a term we use for the automatic intelligence that's running our body. It's a big learning machine, and it wants *quantity* of life. Its goal is to survive and pass on your DNA. It has one job only, to keep you alive. If you've survived something, it believes that to be a good thing, no matter how painful the experience was emotionally. If you survived it, the unconscious has met its desire and will not want to create anything else. So, as you can see, the main conflict is between your unconscious and your self-conscious. One wants to survive and repeat the past, and the other wants to thrive and experience variety. Does that make sense?"

"Look, I've studied Freud and Jung. I understand these concepts all too well, but it hasn't helped me turn my life around."

"Okay, let me break it down," Vance said. "Your self-conscious believes your current reality (CR) is an unwanted experience it needs to change, and that there's an action you need to take to create a desired reality (DR) that is different and better. "

"That sounds about right," Mike said as he drew in his book
Self Conscious Focus

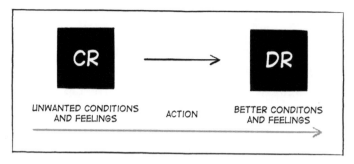

"But as you know, creating what we desire isn't as easy as it looks. This is because our unconscious wants things to stay the same. It views the current reality of unwanted feelings and conditions as good, because you're alive. It doesn't want anything else, so a conflict is created. One wants to change, and the other doesn't. The unconscious focuses on a wound from childhood that it wants to avoid. Its desired reality is to recreate the wound and survive from it. Over and over again. Mike drew the unconscious focus in his book

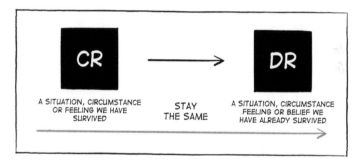

Can you see the conflict?" Vance asked pausing to let Mike catch up. Mike nodded.

"Because of this conflict, most people live in oscillation, back and forth, like being on a swing. As soon as you move toward changing, the part of you that doesn't want to change takes over and ensures you retreat back to where you started."

"Okay, hold on. You're saying the unconscious doesn't want to change, and this is the same for everybody, so we just put up with it?" Mike asked, disgusted. "That doesn't make any sense to me at all. It's the opposite of everything I believe in. Everyone can change. It happens all the time!"

"You're misunderstanding me. Of course we're all capable of change, we're just doing it the wrong way, by fixing instead of shifting our conscious structure.

"So, my unconscious is slowing me down, because it's at war with the other two?"

"The unconscious is actually not the villain here, even though it's been the enemy of the personal development world for years. It's an important ally in creating everything we want. Once we understand how it works, we can use it to create success with ease."

"I'm listening," Mike replied.

"As I said, the unconscious is the part of us that's designed to keep the body alive. It runs your body for you during your formative years, and it learns how to ensure you survive. This means the unconscious learns and creates our programming, and once it's learned something, it doesn't need to relearn it. Instead, it becomes an automated process. This is why you don't have to consciously remember how to talk, even though you first learned it as a toddler. Once your unconscious learns a certain behaviour, it can be quite hard to change, like an accent. Can you imagine how difficult life would be if we didn't have this part of us learning how to do things on autopilot?"

"Yeah, I get it," Mike said, calming down.

"The downside is, the unconscious has no filter. It's an unstoppable learning machine. Anything that threatens your survival, becomes super important to it. It doesn't care about being happy or living with abundance or feeling joy. It cares about being alive. So, for instance, let's say you had a critical parent or grew up in poverty, and you didn't die. The unconscious learns this experience is survivable, and therefore, trying to change your circumstances is a risk it's not willing to take."

"What you're saying is that if you survive living in financial scarcity or being overweight, your unconscious will want you to remain in that reality?"

"Right. Because the unconscious desires to create more experiences similar to what you've already survived, you never get what your self-conscious wants to create. Most people spend their life chasing the dream but never having it. This is why so many athletes, actors, musicians, or lotto winners end up broke after making millions of dollars. They don't consciously try to become broke, but they somehow find a way back to how it always was for them. It seems like they're attracted back to being broke, but it's just structure. It's always structure."

"I've understood these concepts on a clinical level for some time. Like how our world is shaped by our family, associates, and birth order, and how it correlates to our success, or lack thereof. I've even worked with veterans and abuse victims who continue to carry around the pain they experienced and wind up clouding their reality. This was another reason I went into psychology. To see if I could finally let go of the pain of losing my parents. I guess I never associated any of this with how I was living my life and the choices I was making. Probably because it's unconscious, right?"

"Right, because you were a helpless child who lost his family and needed to be saved to survive an unconscious wound was created. Your structure is that you recreate what happened to you as a child by being financially helpless, believing you will be abandoned by your family and hoping to be saved by someone else."

"But, Vance," Mike said angrily. "I *was* a helpless kid who lost his parents. That wasn't my fault! I did need to be saved."

"Please don't be angry at me. I'm simply helping you realize that your unconscious is replaying that experience to this day. To give you more recent examples, you've allowed noisy neighbours to kill your business, you have no way to pay your grandmother's medical bill, and just today, you wanted to enrol me in the same pattern."

Mike sighed. "I can see your point. In my clinic, I constantly work with people who are having the same experience with a co-worker or spouse that they had with a mother or father growing up. It's like we keep playing the same movie again and again."

"Yes!" Vance yelled enthusiastically. "Don't beat yourself up. Most are stuck in the same way. Some people are always sick, because they got attention from their parents. Some of us learned to always keep busy, or never speak up, or never be attractive, because it helped us escape pain. There's an endless number of ways we crazy humans create beliefs and rules about how we should be and what we need to do to avoid pain. The real problem is that because we know how to survive these painful wounding experiences, we continue creating them. How many times in your life have you wanted something, only to conclude there was no way to have it?"

Mike took a breath. "More times than I want to admit," he replied. "When I was a teenager, my dream was to become a rock star, but I gave it up out of fear, just when we were about to make it big."

"That sounds pretty typical, you are like most people and have both the unconscious and self-conscious pulling on your current reality. This creates oscillation. Let me draw out the full structure in your book. " Vance said. Mike handed him the book. Vance grabbed the book and pen and started scribbling.

Vance handed the book back to Mike who studied the diagram.

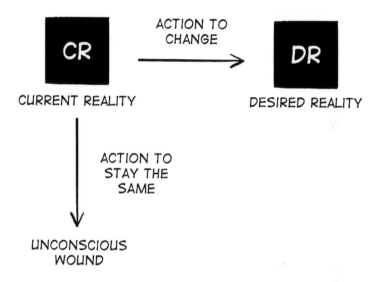

"Now let's make it relevant to you. Let's draw out your personal life structure" Vance said

"Let's start with the self conscious focus to create a better life. Under DR **have enough money and be powerful.** Under CR please write **powerless victim never enough money.** Between those two write the action to change, **create a successful business.** Beneath the current reality please write in the Unconscious wound of **losing family and being powerless.** Between those points write the unconscious action to stay the same which is to **be saved and feel powerless**

Mike did what he was told

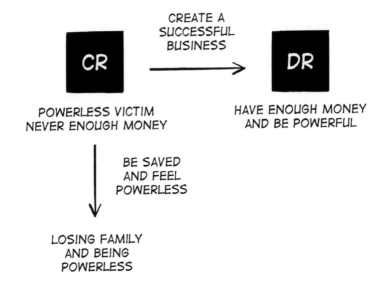

"Can you see the conflict?" Vance asked.

"Yes, but to be honest, I'm a little insulted by the phrase 'powerless victim.' Life has thrown me some curveballs, but I'm dealing with it."

"Mike, I know this is difficult. but if you're constantly look-ing for someone else to save you, even though you really don't want to, and if you're using medication to prevent yourself from feeling frustrated and anxious, then I'd say you've given up your power to something outside of yourself. We need to bring your power back to you."

"Wait, how do you know I'm on medication?" Mike asked.

"It's my superconscious superpower. When you grow up around a father like mine, you're hypersensitive to any addic-tions or dependencies. I assume you had a psychiatrist friend write you a script after a self-diagnosis? I'm not trying to shame you here. I get it. I'm just illustrating a point."

Mike bowed his head. "It's pathetic, isn't it? A psychologist who helps others put their life together, and here I am taking drugs to cope. I'm a total imposter. So, how do we fix it?"

"Ha! That's a great question. And the answer is...you don't! You learn to neutralize it and let go of the wound. You can then shift onto a different path in life, the superconscious path, where you use all three aspects of your consciousness together. Remember, your unconscious is not your enemy. It just received some incorrect training. On the superconscious path, you live in the creative structure, choose what you want to experience or create, and then allow your superconscious to come up with ways of making it happen."

"But how do you fight that unwillingness to change?"

"You don't. Remember, it's not your enemy. We would be in a lot of trouble as a species if we didn't have a part of us totally focused on surviving. The problem isn't with the unconscious, it's the structure. The structure is created by your focus. To change your focus the first thing we must do is neutralize the unconscious wound. It's time to let it go."

CHAPTER FIVE

THE TRUTH

A s Mike watched the children at play, Vance continued his lesson.

"The unconscious is truly the key to having what you want. It's like a magnet for what it believes is the safest reality for us to experience. We'll never have anything if it contradicts our unconscious." He chuckled. "I know this sounds crazy, but a highly successful friend of mine who made millions of dollars in his thirties, and had enough money for four or five lifetimes, struggled to just enjoy life and have fun. He told me he always felt guilty for having all that freedom. It was like some sort of violation."

Mike smiled, feeling a sense of déjà vu "Sometimes I get that way. Like if I have some spare time, I think I'm forgetting to do something important."

"Yes. This is because the unconscious has convinced you that working hard and struggling is safe. For my friend, having freedom and abundance went against what he learned was safe and survivable. The unconscious felt threatened. He thought he was losing his connection to his family, and he started making decisions that sabotaged his success."

"So, his unconscious tried to bring him back to safety, thinking that's what was best for his survival?"

Vance nodded. "Our unconscious has been learning what's safe and survivable from the moment we take our first breath. Many events that weren't perceived on a self-conscious level were recorded in the unconscious in great detail. Like, for example, you don't remember when you first learned to talk, but your unconscious does, right?"

"I guess so," Mike replied.

"But it also learned a lot more. In fact, the unconscious has a huge wealth of memories that you're not aware of, and is always asking, 'How do I survive this situation?' Using its recorded information, it figures out what action it should take. So, if your unconscious believes that life is hard and you're powerless, you will constantly find ways to create that experience.

As your unconscious learns to survive, it taps into the superconscious and acquires a specific superpower. I'll get more into that later, but first, let's concentrate on your current creation, which is the reason you came to me in the first place. We need to neutralize the wound.

Mike nodded.

"What's your greatest fear? Would it be failing to pay for your grandmother's care?" Vance asked

"I guess."

"If that did happen, what would be the consequences?"

"It would be horrible. They would put her on medication that makes her slow and drowsy, and she would need a different place to live." Mike replied.

"Okay, and where would she live?" Vance pressed.

"Probably in our spare room."

"Got it. So, Mike, this is a big question," Vance said before taking a deep breath. "Can you accept the reality of not coming up with the money and the consequences that follow?"

"No, it would be devastating, and she deserves so much better. There's no way I can accept it."

"Why not? Is there anything that would be good about it?"

"No.

"Think harder," Vance insisted.

Mike paused before responding. "Well... I guess she would be around us and the kids more," Mike said reluctantly. "But that's beside the point. She needs the best care, Vance! If your idea of solving this is just to have her come live with us, you clearly don't understand how important it is for me to look after my family. She's all I've got!" Mike yelled, fighting back tears.

"All you've got?" Vance asked, his tone even.

"Yes, it's why I'm here with my hat in my hand trying to figure this out. I have to look after her, especially after all she's done for me."

"Yes, I know, Mike. And you will," Vance replied. "Once you understand how to use the creative power of your superconscious, you will magically create exactly what you desire. The important first step is to become completely neutral about the worst-case scenario, so you don't give it any power." He fixed Mike with a serious look. "So, what's the worst case?" Vance asked again.

"The worst case is I wouldn't get the money to pay for Nana's care. She would have to come live with us or move to a different home, and she would continue on subpar medication," Mike responded.

"What's so bad about that?"

"Weren't you listening? She's frail and needs constant care!"

"Yes, I get it, but what would it mean for you if you couldn't make it happen?"

Mike was becoming more and more frustrated. This conversation appeared to be going nowhere. But he collected his thoughts and said, "It would mean I'd failed."

"Failed?"

"Yes! I would have failed to provide her with the life she deserves and my promise to Pop. I would let them all down. I would be a failure."

"And how does that make you feel?"

"Oh, you're using psychology language on me now? Well, okay, I'll bite. It would make me feel worthless, I can never accept letting her down after all she did for me!"

"So, I would assume these thoughts consume your waking hours?"

"Yes. I'm one-hundred-percent focused on ensuring I don't fail. It's affected every area of my life. I've put on weight, and I hardly spend any time with my kids. I've been working overtime, trying desperately to sell houses, fix the noise problem at the clinic, and service patients. It's a real struggle. I haven't done anything fun for years, and my poor wife, she gets the worst of it," Mike shook his head. "I could fix everything with enough money, but I seem to be getting further and further away. And to be honest, that fifty thousand you offered earlier is looking really tempting right now."

Vance smiled. "Yes, our old patterns are always there to tempt us back to our old structures. It takes willpower to stay focused. I'm proud of you, Mike, and I want to help. Let's get you fully concentrated on what you want, instead of worrying about your supposed failure, because by doing that, you're limiting your creative power."

"Okay," Mike replied far less confidently.

"You have to get completely okay with failing. Otherwise, the fear will take away your creative power from the end result. This should be your sole focus on all levels of consciousness, because what you plant will grow. You can't grow an abundant forest by planting seeds of doubt. Right now, at least fifty percent of your creative power is being taken up by worry and fear. That's what you're planting into your consciousness, and that's what's growing."

Mike rolled his eyes. "Thanks for the botany lesson."

"Please keep an open mind. If structure creates the path of least resistance, your focus creates the structure. As I said, to get different results, you need to change the structure. Because you have a heightened fear of failure and letting your family down, that's where your focus is and not on the desired result." Vance puts his hand on Mike's shoulder. "Would you agree that this method has gotten you nowhere to this point?"

"Yes," Mike replied with a sigh.

"Okay, so to neutralize this thought pattern, you need to become okay with the worst-case scenario. I have a little closed-eye visualization that will help you with this. Even if we can reduce the fear a little, it will help get more of your focus on what you want, which will dramatically increase your creative power, as well as your probability of generating what you desire."

Mike shrugged. "I'm willing to give it a try."

"Great. Now, close your eyes."

Mike did as he was told.

"I want you to visualize the worst-case scenario. Imagine a moment in the future where you can't get the money, and you have to face up to the truth. Your grandmother has to move in with you, and can't get the proper medications. Your clinic fails, you have to close the real estate business, and you can't pay for your daughter's braces. You have to fess up to your wife that it didn't work out, and you have to go back to a government job. Can you do that?"

"I don't know. I feel like I'm going to throw up just thinking about it."

Vance laughed. "It's okay. Just sit in that visualization for a while."

Mike opened his eyes. "I can't do it."

"That's okay," Vance replied. "Let me tell you a quick story. When I was in physical therapy after my discharge from the army, I was solely focused on the fear that I may never walk again. I was frustrated and stressed, yelling at the nurses and pushing everyone away. This stress raised my cortisol, which decreased my ability to heal. Getting upset about a possible failure didn't change the reality that it might happen. In fact, it increased the possibility. The only way to heal was to accept the outcome that I may never walk again and find a way to still be happy. By letting go of the fear, I pulled the power back to myself, which allowed me to focus on what needed to be done. And the rest is history. I was walking in just a few months after that." He smiled. "Worrying about failure could actually cause the failure to happen. And more quickly."

"So, by concentrating on all of the bad outcomes and getting worked up about it, I'm wasting my creative power?"

"Now you're getting it. If you put all of your creative focus on what you want, it's more likely you'll make it happen. We've been taught to focus on what we don't want and avoid it, which never works. Instead, it's crucial to become okay with a negative outcome, realize you can still be happy, and choose to be more powerful than failure. Then you get your power back."

"It's true. The more I try not to think about all of the terrible outcomes, the worse it gets."

"And look, the bad outcome can still happen. But if you remain fully focused on what you truly want, even if you end up in a negative outcome, you'll discover it's not that bad. You'll find a way to be happy, which makes you powerful and allows you to get back to creating what you want. It is time to let go of all this worry. It doesn't help at all."

Mike started to respond but was interrupted by a loud shriek from behind them. A mother was pulling a Labrador puppy away from a toddler with an ice cream cone. As the kid moved to avoid the dog, the ice cream fell off and was now covered in sand. The puppy was wriggling like crazy to get a lick of its newfound delicacy. Everyone found it funny except for the kid, who received a lesson in how close to let a puppy get to your ice cream. They watched as the toddler's mother tied the puppy to a tree and set about cleaning up the mess.

"Ha! Magic!" Vance exclaimed.

Mike was confused. "What are you talking about? That poor kid lost her ice cream."

"I'm talking about the dynamics of the situation. The puppy felt no resistance to having what it wanted. It behaved like the self-conscious, focused on the end result. Its owner behaved like the unconscious and made the final decision based on a fear of cleaning up puppy diarrhea and created a stuck resistance structure by tying the puppy to the tree. This is exactly what happens to us. We learn at an early age what we're allowed to have or not, and create stuck structures that remain unchanged. We use negative feelings like guilt, fear, and worry to tie ourselves to the tree and not go for what we want. Have you ever seen a dog feel guilty or worry about judgment and failure? Even if I've said no to taking my beagle on a walk or throwing the ball, he keeps asking again and again. There's something to learn from that, isn't there?"

"I guess," Mike replied.

"So, Mike, what do you really want? If you could be like that puppy before you learned what was right or wrong, or what was possible or impossible, if you could have anything in the world you desired, what would it be?"

Without pausing Mike responded, "I would want my parents back. It's so unfair that they were killed."

"Yes, exactly," said Vance. "This desire rules your life and is creating massive oscillation and conflict inside of you, because it's based on an unconscious wound. It was so painful for you to lose your parents, your unconscious decided it would do everything to avoid this experience again. But in order to avoid something, that something must exist. The reason you continue recreating this experience is that your unconscious knows exactly what to do to survive. In fact, you're so good at creating the experience of being abandoned by family, you're unconsciously constructing scenarios where you're about to lose them and be financially dependent on others. Your sole focus on your grandmother has fractured your relationship with your wife and children, hasn't it?

Mike nodded. "It's what keeps me up at night."

"Remember, we can live in one of two structures that are quite different and usually conflicting. The creative structure is driven by your self-conscious desire to have a good life, like the puppy, while the problem structure is driven by your unconscious to ensure your survival and safety, like the puppy's owner. You could just tell your nana that the insurance won't cover her treatment, and you can't afford to keep her in the home, but you don't, because you fear that telling her the truth will mean you'll lose her. This is way too painful to admit, so you stress out, causing yourself health problems, and by pushing your family away, you're manifesting the very result you fear. Your whole orientation in life is based on what you don't want."

"Yes, Vance, I'm well aware of this. Most people who lose their parents at a young age are traumatized. I've been to many therapists and healers, and even tried hypnotherapy to get rid of the anxiety of being abandoned again. I've been trying my whole life to let this go. I've received multiple degrees and spent thousands on courses. I chant affirmations every morning, try to think positively, and read as many books on personal development as possible. I've looked into different religions and taken advanced consciousness training. I've changed my diet, gone to retreats, and taken all sorts of drugs. I've tried it all. Nothing works long-term. I always have this fear that I'm about to have it all taken away from me."

"Great. So, you're ahead of the game. You know what doesn't work. I can tell you what does."

"Really? You think you know better than all of these people how to fix my childhood trauma?" Mike said sarcastically. "What could you possibly tell me that I haven't already learned?"

"I can teach you a lot, actually," Vance said, tossing off Mike's sarcasm. "First, I want you to know how sorry I am for your loss. It sure was a terrible time for you."

"Thank you," Mike said sincerely.

"Second, nearly everyone faces big challenges. There are people who've had it much worse than you, and some who've had it much better. However, everyone finds a way to feel like they missed out on something. It's a common theme."

"So, you're telling me I'm not special," Mike said with a smile.

"Hardly," Vance said, grinning. "The third thing I want you to know is that by focusing on the problem, you will never get rid of it, because you're in a stuck reality. In order for you to fix a problem, you must first experience it as something you don't want, and then come up with solutions you believe will get rid of it, until it becomes all that you know. Your problem is your safe harbor, and your unconscious will never allow you to be fully rid of it. This is why you, and many others, try countless therapies to try and fix the problem, only to find yourself in the same position. Most of the world lives in the problem orientation and structure, which is the complete opposite of the creative orientation and structure, where your focus should be.

Mike sat there taking it all in. Then, he turned to Vance. "Okay, I think I understand what you mean. The unconscious wants to keep you alive, so it remembers all your pain and wants to avoid it, right?" Mike asked.

"Yep."

Mike nodded. "But to solve the problem, the unconscious has to constantly experience what it doesn't want to feel, so it can avoid it, meaning it can never fully let it go."

"Yes, it's some crazy logic, but there you go," Vance said, laughing.

"Okay, and if I concentrate totally on creating what I desire, without any focus on what I don't want, I'm more likely to have it, because I'm using all of my power?"

"That's it!" Vance said. "Are you ready to let go of the fear of the worst-case scenario now?"

"I'm willing to give it a try." Mike replied.

"Okay, let's start again. Close your eyes and visualize the worst case happening. Really build a full sensory experience of it. Notice what you see, feel, hear, think, and do. Sit in that experience and just breathe,"

Mike closed his eyes and pictured it all going wrong, owning the failure of not coming up with the money and feeling it. After a minute or so, Vance asked, "Now that you're visualizing it, do you notice one thing that's actually good about this experience?"

After a few more moments, Mike responded, "Honestly, I can. Nana would be close to her family. I would have a low-pressure, nine-to-five job, which means I'd have my weekends back. I would stop being stressed and would probably have more energy to go to the gym, play music, and reconnect with June."

Vance nodded. "That all sounds great."

"The one thing I can't let go of is my nana not receiving the care she needs."

"Yes, that would be terribly unfortunate," said Vance. "So, close your eyes again."

Mike closed his eyes.

"I want you to release all of the upset emotion from this situation. Guilt and worry won't help you create a different reality. Now, visualize a moment where you're experiencing your nana not receiving the care she needs and growing frailer. Hold this image, until you can accept this reality could happen, and even though it's not at all ideal, just acknowledge that aging is part of the human process. Notice the good of having your nana with her family. Bring the power back to yourself. If this situation happened, how might you accept it and then turn it around? Allow yourself to trust your own ability and release this pressure on yourself. Do you have that image in your head?"

"Yes," Mike said with some emotion.

"Now, open your eyes and tell me what you've learned."

"Well, I understand how this may happen, and it's not what I want, but in terms of some of my problems, like my business neighbours, there's no point in putting any energy into it. If it happens, it happens, but my worry isn't doing anything to stop it." He sighed. "And actually, there is a situation that's worse than my original worst-case."

"Please, tell me about it."

"It's something I may have wound up creating if you weren't doing this with me today. That would be wasting my life worrying and stressing about finding the money, while neglecting time with my family. Like you said, I was doing everything I could to ensure I looked after everyone, but this was only speeding up the process of what I feared the most, and that's losing them. And what's worse, I'm missing out on quality time with Nana. She's getting up there in age, and I'm spending the few years she has left on worrying about her."

"Now that's some food for thought!" Vance said. "And speaking of food, are you hungry? I'm starving. Let's grab some lunch."

Mike looked at his watch. It was nearly one p.m. He'd been talking to this famous billionaire for nearly three hours!

"Sounds good to me!" Mike replied.

Vance pulled out his phone and called his driver. They'd walked quite a distance, so Mike was happy about this. Mike wrote in his book, *You must become ok with the worst-case scenario*. Within a few moments, the black Rolls Royce pulled up, and they got in.

As they drove, Mike started feeling guilty about how he'd treated Vance, who'd given him so much of his valuable time.

"Vance, I'm so grateful for this morning. Sorry if I was rude to you. It's been a stressful few months. I think I've had a real breakthrough. You see, for years I was trying to change how I feel about my parents' death. The truth is, even with all the work I've done, I still haven't come to grips with it. I never really considered that by focusing on trying to change or heal that feeling, I was recreating it over and over again, conditioning my unconscious to relive it even more. If I'd focused on what I wanted, their death would have become a distant memory, instead of a ball and chain I carry around with me. Now I've given these feelings so much power, I'm living in fear of abandonment and constantly believe I'm on the brink of losing them, which my logical mind knows isn't true".

"I'm glad you understand this on an intellectual level, the trick is putting it into practice. Let's say you're starting from scratch. As of this moment, how would you create your life? What's in your heart?"

"Well, that's easy. I would love to have a happy and healthy family," Mike responded. before laughing and adding, "and make shitloads of money."

Vance chuckled along with him. "That all sounds great. What else?"

Mike paused to think and then blurted, "I would also love to play music and maybe join a band."

"Okay, great start. Write those down," Vance instructed.

Mike grabbed his pen and wrote them down.

"Now comes the fun part. We get to reorient you into the creative structure that will put you on the superconscious path, one that's guided by your true choices, where you take intuitive action. Your life is about to become magical!" Vance said enthusiastically. Then on a more serious note, he added, "The biggest challenge will be to stay on the path when the end result really matters to you. Regarding those outcomes about a happy and healthy family, playing in a band, and creating loads of money, how long have you had these aspirations?" Vance asked.

"Well, my whole life, I guess. Except playing in the band. I just threw that in there as a joke. It's a silly childhood dream. What matters is the family and the money," Mike responded.

"Okay, so where are you now compared to what you would like to create?"

"Well, as you know, I'm trying to make the money, and I'm not getting anywhere. My family is healthy except for Nana, but there isn't much I can do about that, and I guess they're all happy. And as I said, the band thing was a joke. I should take it off the list," Mike said as he went to cross it out.

Vance stuck his hand out to stop him. "Wait a second. When I asked you to compare your present life to your desired one, how did you feel?"

Mike didn't want to admit this, but he knew he had to be honest. "I guess I felt powerless. It all feels impossible, and I kind of just hoped other people would take care of it." He punched his thigh. "Dammit, even I can see where my focus is" Mike replied in frustration.

"Exactly! That's great awareness and a huge step in the right direction. One more thing. Did you notice how you're talking yourself out of playing in a band? You clearly want to, but it seems on some level, you believe you're not allowed to do something for yourself. I want you to leave that on your list. You're either all in or not, remember? If you give power to a belief that you can't have what you want, you're giving in to the unconscious agenda. Stepping onto the superconscious path and creating magical results is going to be the best thing you ever do, but as I said, it's going to take courage. You're the only one who can truly ensure you stay on the path.

"That sounds great. I already feel inspired to create this life."

"Actually, Mike, generating desire is the easy part. Learning to construct a completely different reality that's in contrast to your unconscious beliefs, is where you'll face all the conflict. You see, if we were to focus on having an enjoyable lunch together right now, it's easy. There's nothing at stake. We have no unconscious resistance to it. We don't really care if we fail, right?"

Mike nodded. "That's true."

"But when it comes to creating a new reality that's nothing like your past, it's much harder. As soon as we choose to go for what we really want, our unconscious creates feelings and beliefs to throw us off track. This is what just happened to you. It's a protection mechanism, designed to keep things the same."

"Yeah, it immediately felt wrong and like I needed to run for safety."

"I get that. If you want something different, you must train yourself to stay focused on the end result and follow through. If you hold your focus on the desired result and notice where you are in comparison, it creates a structure that causes a tension or discrepancy between where you are and where you want to be. Your superconscious superpower is then activated, so you find creative ways to make it happen. Like I said before, my superpower is sensing when someone's hiding things. We all have a superpower and we can tap into it to produce magical results! How great is that!?" Vance asked, grinning ear to ear.

"That sounds amazing!" Mike said as the driver pulled to the side of the road. They were stopped in a loading zone, and an angry truck driver was already on his horn behind them.

"Quick! Jump out!" Vance said.

Before Mike knew it, Vance was already halfway out of the car and ushering Mike to join him.

Mike got out and looked around, feeling disoriented. This part of town was dead. They were standing next to an abandoned industrial building with boarded-up windows. On the other side of the road was a car scrap yard and some empty buildings. But strangely, parked cars lined both sides of the street, and there was a huge line of people coming out of an alleyway just ahead of them for no obvious reason. Mike saw no evidence of a restaurant, but up by the line of people, there was a buzzing red-neon sign that read *Chow*.

Mike had been salivating, thinking they were going to one of Vance's restaurants. This wasn't at all what he expected. "Where are we? Is there a restaurant out here?"

"Yes. It's called Chow. Have you ever been?" Vance asked.

"No," Mike replied. "Never."

"Well, you're in for a treat, then. It's only the best sushi in the state," Vance said as they walked toward the building.

"If there's a line of people out the door on a Friday afternoon, this place must be amazing."

Vance confidently walked past everyone and went right to the front of the line. The greeter at the door had a big smile on his face.

"Mr. Vanderhill, great to see you," he said.

"Hey, Jimmy, you guys look quiet today," Vance said with a smile.

"It's nonstop".

"Jimmy, meet Mike. He'll be dining with me today. Do you have room for two?"

"For you, sir, anything," Jimmy replied, ushering Mike and Vance into the building. "Right this way."

Mike couldn't help but feel pride being in the company of Vance.

As they went down the dark, carpeted corridor, Mike noted the contrast from their sunny morning at the beach. When they reached the end, there was a big, heavy wooden door that opened to an eruption of sound as they entered the busy restaurant. Mike was stunned.

The place was dimly lit but full of energy. There were five sushi chefs lined up in a row, putting on a performance and creating sushi right in front of the bar. Waitstaff bustled around the tables, delivering all sorts of steaming delicacies. Mike could see there was much more than just sushi on offer.

Looking to the upstairs floors, Mike saw private rooms filled with people singing karaoke, and even though it was only the middle of the day, it looked like some of them were already three sheets to the wind.

They were shown to their table, which was in a roped-off VIP section up one end of the bar.

Mike felt completely out of place, but when he picked up the menu, the panic really set in. He had a pang of *I can't afford to eat here* as he looked at the prices. Sixteen dollars per piece of sushi! What an insult. He couldn't believe Vance took him here after a morning of him talking about his financial woes.

"I'll be back in a second," Vance said. "There's someone I'd like you to meet." While Vance was away, Mike searched for something in his price range and noticed the menu had everything he could imagine, from sushi to steak and fries. This place had it all. He'd never been anywhere like it.

A minute later, Vance returned, pulling a young Asian woman by her hand and dodging his way through the crowd.

"Mike, meet Suzi Chow. She owns this place. Suzi, this is Mike Dunne, a friend of mine," Vance said. "Suzi built this place out of nothing, in the middle of nowhere. When I met her, she was stuck working long hours in her father's accountancy firm."

"Hi, Suzi, nice to meet you. From the street, I never would have guessed all of this was going on."

"I know, right!" she said with enthusiasm. "I basically got this place for free. The rent was so cheap. I just love it. In fact, it was a superconscious creation that seemed impossible at the time."

"So, what's the cuisine? I can see all sorts of dishes. Is it Japanese? And is that karaoke upstairs?" Mike asked, genuinely interested.

"Yes, it's karaoke and yes, the cuisine is unique, a bit of everything. As long as it's premium," Suzi replied. "In fact, Chow is always changing. What you see on the menu is everything I'm excited about right now. The food, music, style, I just love it. I like to keep it fresh and exciting. If you come back in a month, eighty percent of the menu will be different, as well as the music, and even the tablecloths. I was thinking a real gothic theme would be next. This New York hipster vibe is getting old," she said with a smile.

Mike looked around the bustling restaurant. It sure was different. "That must be what keeps people coming back."

Suzi nodded. "Definitely. The only constants are the location, staff, and level of service, but the food and vibe are on constant rotation. Keeping things new and fresh is my life-blood. Can you imagine I used to be an accountant?"

Mike was still catching up to the whirlwind of stepping into Chow. "No, you seem way too enthusiastic and vibrant to be stuck behind a desk in some cubicle, crunching numbers. What caused the change?"

"It's crazy what we do when we're living in the problem structure. Both my parents are first-generation immigrants to this country. As a child, I saw them working so hard, there was never any time for play. Then when I grew up, I became an accountant, because I wanted to please my father, who'd always wanted me to follow in his footsteps. In my off hours, I was constantly traveling, starting new projects, and learning new things, while at work I kept to myself."

"Yeah, I know what that's like. So many people drag themselves to their jobs and only have fun on the weekends or on vacation."

"That was me! And then I met Vance. I was his accountant. We became pretty close, and of course, with his superpower, he knew I wasn't happy. When I finally confided in him, he helped me let go of my unconscious agenda and use the superconscious creation process. After getting my training and consciousness education from Vance, I was able to reignite my superpower and live true to my heart. I owe everything to this man," she said, wrapping her arm around Vance and giving him a squeeze.

"That's incredible," Mike said. "So, what made you come up with the idea for this restaurant?"

"I'd always had this dream of bringing the world to Williamstown. I wanted to fly in fresh fish from Japan and make authentic sushi, with the sounds of Italian tenors and the fresh spices of India all under one roof. I also wanted people to be entertained in a light-hearted atmosphere, where they could sing their hearts out with karaoke morning and night. No one thought it would work, but here we are, three years later. I'm making more money than I ever have, and the best part is, I get to take work trips around the world, getting new inspiration to keep this place fresh."

"It sure is amazing," Mike said. "Well done."

"Honestly, though," she said, leaning over and lowering her voice, "I think for a while, my father wanted to kill Vance for giving me so much confidence. He made my father realize where he'd chosen to deny his own truth. It's easy to do, really. There were many times I wanted to stop and give up. For example, when the pandemic hit, I'd only been open a year or so, and we thought we'd have to close. But using my superpower, I realized this place could have a masquerade theme. We created these beautiful masks that also kept all of our patrons healthy and following the rules. As a result, we were one of the few restaurants thriving through the pandemic, and our sales boomed. We were able to keep our staff and buy from our suppliers. That one idea helped a lot of people."

"Yeah, times were tough back then. A lot of smaller places went under."

"Everyone told me I was crazy. That my idea wouldn't work, and I should close. They were all scared, and I was, too, but I followed the guidance of my superconscious." She shook her head "I wasted so much time denying my true nature. I had the idea for Chow a good ten years before I took the plunge, but I was more worried about failing than living my life in misery. But when I decided to walk the path of a creator and integrate my superconscious superpower..." she expands her arms to indicate the restaurant "...my whole world became brighter."

"I can see what you've manifested and what a big risk it must have been."

"As Vance's accountant, I could see how much he was making in the restaurant industry, and I'd had years of planning and ideas, but I was still so frightened. Then Vance taught me that you have to risk failure to achieve the success your heart desires, so even though I was living in FUD, I went all-in with my natural creative ability."

"FUD?" Mike asked, confused.

"Fear, uncertainty, and doubt are the killers of your super-conscious superpower," Vance and Suzi said in unison, and they burst out laughing.

Mike couldn't help but join in. The joy these two super-successful people exuded was contagious. There was something magical about Suzi. She seemed to have unlimited enthusiasm and energy.

"Wow, Suzi! You're an inspiration. I'm so ready to learn how to become a superconscious creator. If I can have ten percent of the success you two have been able to achieve, I'll be happy," Mike said.

"So, what's your superpower, Mike?" Suzi asked.

"We haven't gotten that far yet," Mike replied, giving Vance a look that suggested he was starting to get impatient.

"Oh, really? You're just starting out on the path?".

"He sure is," Vance said. "Just this morning, he didn't even know what the creative structure was."

"Fresh meat," Suzi said, licking her lips mockingly. "So, you guys just come in for a chat, or are you hungry? What can I get you?"

She pointed to the menus sitting open on the table.

"We sure are!" Vance replied. "But how about you decide? We're both hungry after a morning of intense creative discussion. You get whatever you think is best for us."

"Okay, just the way I like it. I'll have something special made up for you!" Suzi exclaimed, nearly skipping away with excitement.

"And a couple of beers would go down great!" Vance shouted after her.

Mike tried to tally what all of this would cost, and his brain went numb thinking about it. He battled with himself about telling Vance there was no way he could afford a whole bunch of food, plus the beers, but he decided to deal with that when the check came.

Vance urged Mike to move, so they could both sit on the same side of the table as they looked out at the buzzing bar. "This place is remarkable, isn't it?"

"It sure is," Mike replied.

"The best part is that Suzi created this all herself. I'd been using her father's accountants for years, and when I met Suzi, she was doing everything right, but she was miserable. One day when I met with her, she was visibly stressed and upset. She'd broken up with her fiancé, was having health problems, and just had a big fight with her father."

"Wow, that does sound tough," Mike said.

"Like many people I meet at their lowest point, that day was transformational for her. Instead of our normal accounting meeting, it became her first lesson in conscious education. After I taught her about the structure and the unconscious, I asked her what she would really love to create. Her answer was that she wanted to have the taste of Japan here in Williamstown, to do something for herself, and most important of all, to feel on purpose and alive. But she thought it was all impossible. Her health condition and controlling father were holding her back. She was so critical of herself and had many speed bumps along the way, but she held her focus and created this extraordinary life! She's now in a new relationship, healthy and happy, with a beautiful one-year-old baby boy at home. I'm so proud of her," Vance said lovingly.

Within minutes, Suzi was back with two beers and a big smile on her face.

"Here you go," she said. "Wait till you see what I've ordered for you."

"So, you fly the fish in daily?" Mike asked. "That must get expensive!"

Suzi smiled. "When I first came up with the idea, everyone told me I was crazy. And because I'm trained as an accountant, my brain kept telling me it didn't make financial sense. But I just had to trust my superconscious intuition. I knew how much better sushi tasted in Japan, due to the freshness and quality of the meat, so I decided to go for it. I wasn't sure people would pay enough to make the cost worth it, but it's become the biggest talking point for Chow. It's actually the only thing on the menu that doesn't change. I know on paper, the revolving menu of dishes from every continent and having five high-quality sushi chefs, not to mention a separate full kitchen staff and karaoke, seems ridiculous, but here we are!"

"Hey, you can't argue with success," Mike said.

"I mean, it's ridiculous. It shouldn't work, but it does. You just have to trust the power of your superconscious." She laughed. "I'm kind of jealous that you're just getting started. I can't wait to talk to you after you've learned from the master." She sighed happily. "Well, I'm off to get your food!"

And with that final word, she danced away again.

CHAPTER SIX

THE MAGNETIC MIND

"Cheers," Vance said to Mike, grabbing a beer.

"Cheers," Mike replied and took a sip. "I understand why you brought me here. If Suzi's an example of what your lessons can bring about, I'm here for it!"

"Suzi has the superpower of enthusiasm and ideas. She bubbles over with more excitement every day than most have in a lifetime. However, it also has its dark side, just like all of the nine orientation points."

"Orientation point?" Mike asked.

"An orientation point is how our consciousness is focused. There are nine orientation points, each with an unconscious wound and superconscious superpower. Suzi lives from the seventh orientation point and is happiest when she is creating new ideas and excitement."

"I can see how purely happy she is. She's doing what she loves, and she seems totally present for it."

"Mike, every one of us starts out as pure consciousness. As we come into human form, we're unable to do much of anything for ourselves and rely on others. When we get older, if we feel our needs aren't being met, it creates a wounding experience, and we form a belief that we must do something to overcome it. Because we have no logical thinking mind yet, we use our superconscious intuition to form strategies that help us overcome the perceived loss. This is how our super-conscious superpower comes into our consciousness."

"So, my parents dying when I was young, created a wounding experience? And that created a superpower?"

"That's right."

Mike blew out a breath.

"Get your notebook out. I want to draw this out for you." Vance instructed.

Mike took out his notebook and handed it to Vance..

"We all start out as pure creative energy. Then we are born into our human experience, which is our vehicle to express our true nature and purpose. We desire to know how it is in this world so we can survive and thrive. Throughout this process our unconscious experiences the pain of needs not being met fully which creates a wound. Because of this wound we create unconscious and superconscious compensating strategies to avoid it happening again." Vance handed the book back to Mike who looked down at what was written

PURE CREATIVE
ENERGY

↓

ENTERS VEHICLE
OF EXPRESSION

↓

DESIRES TO KNOW HOW IT IS
(SEEKS TO THRIVE AND SURVIVE)

↓

WOUNDING EXPERIENCE
(UNMEET NEEDS)

↓

CREATE COMPENSATING
STRATEGY

↓

CREATES UNCONSCIOUS
AGENDA & SUPERCONSCIOUS
SUPERPOWER

"Okay, I think I got it," Mike said. "I actually see this a lot in my clinic. I guess since there are nine orientation points, that must mean there are nine wounds and nine compensating strategies that turn into a superconscious superpower?" Mike asked.

"Yes, one-hundred percent," Vance replied. "Now I'd like to talk about the first orientation that has the superpower of perfection. This is the intuitive ability to have discernment and to see things as they could be, in total, beautiful perfection. The downside is that because you see perfection, you also recognize imperfection. If you stay stuck in the wound of this superpower, you could seem judgmental, critical, and downright mean."

"Huh," Mike said. "I think my daughter, Bec, is like that. She's always pointing out how wrong things are, constantly looking to be good and do the right thing but being really critical of herself. She's a talented artist, but she never seems to finish anything she starts, because it's never perfect enough."

"Yes, that's exactly right. All of the nine superpowers have their dark side," Vance said as he grabbed Mike's notebook and drew a strange circular shape with some kind of nine-pointed star in the middle. "This is the enneagram. It's an ancient Sufi teaching that describes nine different unconscious fixations and their interrelationships. The orientation points are both powerful and destructive, with a superpower and a supervillain. As we've discussed, the unconscious has the desire to survive, anytime it feels its survival is threatened, it creates a wound. In order to become powerful creators and walk the superconscious path, we must know our orientation and use our superpower to create magic. The orientations are hard to describe, unless you live from that perspective. I'll try my best by giving common names for them," Vance said, as he kept writing in the notebook. Each point of the star had the numbers one through nine, and he began labelling them.

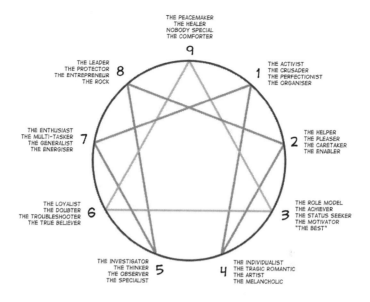

THE PEACEMAKER
THE HEALER
NOBODY SPECIAL
THE COMFORTER
9

THE LEADER
THE PROTECTOR
THE ENTREPRENEUR
THE ROCK
8

THE ACTIVIST
THE CRUSADER
THE PERFECTIONIST
THE ORGANISER
1

THE ENTHUSIAST
THE MULTI-TASKER
THE GENERALIST
THE ENERGISER
7

THE HELPER
THE PLEASER
THE CARETAKER
THE ENABLER
2

THE LOYALIST
THE DOUBTER
THE TROUBLESHOOTER
THE TRUE BELIEVER
6

THE ROLE MODEL
THE ACHIEVER
THE STATUS SEEKER
THE MOTIVATOR
"THE BEST"
3

THE INVESTIGATOR
THE THINKER
THE OBSERVER
THE SPECIALIST
5

THE INDIVIDUALIST
THE TRAGIC ROMANTIC
THE ARTIST
THE MELANCHOLIC
4

"As I mentioned, Suzi associates with the seventh orientational point. The wound of this orientation is that the person is unable to allow any negative feelings. You see, as a child, someone with the seventh power wasn't allowed to feel sad or unhappy, and because of that, doesn't actually know how to process so-called negative feelings. To avoid them, they always have lots of ideas, plans, and interests. Her superconscious superpower is 'the enthusiast.'"

"So, what's mine?"

"The second one. Your wound and corresponding superpower is based on a fear that you're not worthy of receiving love or being needed, and the belief that you must do things for others in order to be loved. What's amazing is that this manifested superpower allows you to create with magic."

Mike was excited to find out what all of this meant and was just about to ask a question, when the people he least wanted to see walked into the bar. They were all in their late thirties, dressed in black, with ripped jeans, Ramones T-shirts, and leather jackets. They looked like they were headed to a Sex Pistols costume party.

"What is it?" Vance asked, knocking Mike out of his trance.

"See that group that just walked in?" Mike said.

"Hard to miss," Vance replied jokingly. "Do you know them?"

"It's my old punk rock band, the Raging Crows. About twenty years ago, I formed the band with three of my best friends from high school. I was the bass player. That big guy is Trevor Hoyer. We called him Big T. He played drums. Bobby Reed, the one with the long hair to his left, was on guitar. The short guy with spiky hair is Jake Rose, the lead singer. He was my best friend from kindergarten to the end of high school. I played bass. Jake's dad gave us the money to make a professional demo."

"That sounds great," Vance said.

"It was, but at the time, I had a big conversation with my grandfather, who convinced me that going to college was a better option than trying to create a career in punk rock."

"Ah, I see. So, you decided to take his advice."

"I always had good grades, so I figured I'd send my transcripts to a few colleges to see what happened. If nobody took the bait, well then, at least I could tell my grandfather I tried. But when I received an acceptance letter, I didn't have the heart to tell the rest of the band, until Jake told me a record company was interested in signing us." Mike sighed. "But if I'm being completely honest with myself, the straw that broke the camel's back was my girlfriend, Jax, suddenly breaking up with me. The woman to Jake's left in the leather pants with the long black hair and blue eyes? That's her. So, they found another bass player and finally hit it big. I haven't seen them in person since."

"What a coincidence. It's magic!" Vance said with enthusiasm. "Let's invite them over! I'd love to meet them."

"No, no, please don't," Mike pleaded. "Vance, there's nothing I regret more than walking away from them. I watched from a distance as the band I started went on to produce hit after hit and single handedly kept punk rock alive in this part of the country. They've been super successful. I always wondered what might have been," Mike said. "Anyway, it would just be so weird."

"Got it," Vance said. Both men looked over as the Raging Crows and supporting cast of rockers found seats in front of the sushi chefs at the other end of the restaurant.

After a few moments, Vance broke the silence. "But is it really what you want?"

"Huh? What?" Mike asked, lost in his own thoughts.

"What do you really want? To never speak to them again or to be friends? Surely, you would have lots to talk about, right?"

"Yeah, I guess, but it was so long ago. I didn't really handle things well back then. I said some pretty hurtful things, to be honest."

"I'm sure you can bury whatever happened in the past. Isn't it worth the risk?" Vance asked.

"Well, honestly, I would love to reconnect with them. I'm so proud of their success. But what would I say?" He sighed. "Hey, guys... sorry I left... Guess it worked out well for you... How's the last twenty years been?" Mike said, mocking himself.

"Well, that's one way of handling it," Vance said in a wry tone. "Let's try something. Remember the process from before? The one where you become okay with failure?"

"Sure," Mike replied.

"Great. It was just a small part of the process that moves you into the creative structure and onto the superconscious path. Now is a good time to practice the rest of it, since you'll use a lot. Once you become okay with the worst-case scenario, the next step is to visualize how you would like it to be. The last step is to ask your superconscious self what action is needed to turn that vision into reality. Does that make sense?"

Mike nodded. "In other words, rather than feeling sorry for myself, I should allow my superpower to take over, so I make the best decision for myself."

"That's the deal. So, what's the worst thing that could happen?" asked Vance.

"They would reject me," Mike replied.

"Okay, close your eyes and experience the rejection happening. Keep visualizing it, until you can accept that reality and find something good about it," Vance instructed.

After a few moments, Mike opened his eyes and said, "The good thing would be that I would have at least tried, and I'd be no worse than I am sitting here right now."

"That's it! So, how would you prefer the experience to go?"

"I would like to reconnect with them, share a beer and a laugh, and put the past behind us. I'd also like to congratulate them on their success and catch up."

"Okay, great. Now close your eyes and create that in your mind. See it happening in perfection, exactly as you would love it to be. Create a full sensory experience of it. Take your time building that in your mind."

Mike closed his eyes and followed instructions. He saw himself laughing and joking with his friends. He imagined hearing himself apologizing for past mistakes and being well-received. It felt good. A big smile spread across his face as he thought about it.

Vance, must have seen his smile, because he said, "What's the next action you must take to create that experience?"

Without hesitation, Mike replied "I should go over and buy them all a drink".

"Okay! Go do it!"

Without thinking, Mike got up and began walking over to the group. As he did, his gaze landed on Jax. Before he dated June, he was head over heels in love with Jax. Mike thought they would be together forever.

There she is, he thought to himself, *Jacqueline Maycroft*. Even after twenty years, she was as beautiful as he remembered.

Of course, he also remembered the times she'd tried to make him jealous, and he'd find out certain details of her stories weren't true. Jax had been a little attracted to drama, but he'd chalked it up to her being a teenage girl and figured they were all like that, until he met June and found out how wrong he was.

As he got closer, fear and anxiety built up in his stomach. All the confidence he'd exhibited at the table had drained from his body, but he didn't want to look like a wimp in front of Vance, so he forced himself to keep going.

When he was about five feet away, he said, "Aren't you the famous Raging Crows?"

The group turned around, expecting some overhyped fan.

"Hi, guys! Fancy bumping into you here," Mike said with the biggest grin and the fakest confidence he could muster.

They all had surprised looks on their faces.

"Dunny... is that you?" Jake exclaimed. "Holy crap, dude, how are you?" he said, before getting up and stretching out his hand to shake.

"I'm great. Are you back in town for long?" Mike asked, gripping his old friend's hand.

"Just for a few days," Bobby replied. "We're here for a gig and heard this was the place to come. I hear you're a big-shot doctor now?" He gave Mike a gentle punch in the stomach.

"Mikey!" Jax shrieked as she pushed through the group to wrap her arms around Mike's neck and plant a big kiss on his cheek. "How long has it been? Must be at least twenty years," she said.

"Yes, I guess it has! Can I buy a round of drinks?" Mike replied.

"Does a bear shit in the woods?" Big T chimed in. "Of course!"

"I can't stay long. I'm in a meeting with Vance Vanderhill over there," he said, pointing to the VIP corner. "But it's so great to see you!"

Big T said, "So, you really are a successful doctor, having meetings with a billionaire in the most exclusive bar in town. Well done, bro." He pulled out a chair. "He can wait a minute for you to catch up with old friends. C'mon, have a seat. We haven't seen you in decades."

"Thanks," Mike said, taking the offered chair. "So, you're in town just for the weekend? You all still live in the big city?"

"Yeah, we're on our ten-year anniversary tour for *Double Barrel*," Bobby replied. "It hit platinum."

"Ah, right! I bought that one. I was so proud."

In fact, Mike was secretly quite envious. He'd purchased each album his old band put out, and in secret, learned to play every song behind closed doors, all the while wishing he'd never left.

But still, he would never trade the life he had. Looking at his old friends, he saw that the years on the road and the rock-and-roll lifestyle had definitely caught up to them. They all looked at least ten years older than their actual age.

"It should have been you playing with us!" Big T exclaimed, loud enough for the whole group to hear. He was never one to beat around the bush.

"Yeah, maybe in another lifetime," Mike replied. "Your bassist that replaced me seems like he's done a really good job."

"Actually, we've gone through about five," Bobby shot back. "We never could find anyone that fit us like you did."

Silence fell over the group as they all ruminated on what might have been.

"So, how are you?" Jake asked.

"Life is great," Mike replied. "I married June Baker. Remember her? We have two kids, twins." Mike awkwardly realized that he hadn't even invited his childhood best friends to the wedding, or even tried to contact them. Changing the subject quickly, he said, "I run a small psychology clinic, and our house is about three blocks from where I used to live with Nana and Pop!"

"Wow, the American dream," Jax said with a hint of sarcasm. "Sounds like you really got it all figured out in the end. I guess you made the right decision about going to college."

Mike needed another change of subject, fast. "So, guys, what have you all been doing besides music?" Mike asked.

"Well..." Jake replied, taking a big breath. "Jax and I got married a few years ago. We have four children and moved out to the countryside. We live just past the racetrack. It's actually closer to Williamstown than the big city."

The whole group looked over to see how Mike would react to hearing his old best friend had married his high school sweetheart. But Mike was determined to stay poker-faced, even though it did sting a little.

"Wow, that's a great place to live," Mike said.

"Sure is," Jax said. "We've been semi-retired for a few years now, mainly living off the royalties, as well as a little music-teaching business on the side. Bobby's made his home in the city and owns the best small live music venue in the state. And Big T is still growing up." She laughed.

"Still growing up? I'm the biggest one here!" Big T objected. "Mike, don't listen to her, I'm doing great. I'm a motorcycle mechanic, and unlike these old farts, rock and roll hasn't died in me yet," he said, poking fun at the others.

"What Jax means is old Trevor here is working his way through all the good-looking rockers of our era and has five kids from four different women," Jake said.

"That we know of..." Bobby added.

The group laughed.

"You never had a problem with the ladies, Trev," Mike said.

The waiter brought over their beers. Mike handed over his credit card, praying the payment would go through, and was relieved when the waiter returned with the bill for him to sign.

He held up his glass and said, "Cheers! It sure is great to see you. I wish I had more time to spend with you guys, but I should get back to my meeting. I'm in a bit of a challenging situation with Nana, and Vance over there is helping me figure it out. When's your gig? Maybe I can pop in and see you."

"We're playing tomorrow night at The Revolver down on Tory Street. If you'd like to come, we'll leave your name at the door," Jake replied.

"Yes, I would love to," Mike lied.

Jax's enthusiastic reply caught Mike by surprise. "Great, we'll see you there. It will be like old times!"

"See you!" Mike said, while grabbing his beer.

Turning to make his way back through the crowd, he could see the billionaire was already enjoying a selection of sizzling-hot dishes and had been joined by two people.

Wow, Mike thought to himself. *Jax and Jake got married. I never saw that coming. They wouldn't have even known each other if it wasn't for me.* A weird feeling came over Mike that wasn't quite jealousy. Maybe it was regret, or relief, or a sense of what might have been.

Mike sat down at the table with Vance, ready to finally eat.

"How did it go?" Vance asked.

"Exactly as I envisioned it," Mike replied.

"Magic," Vance said with a wink. "Mike, I want you to meet two successful superconscious creators, Nikola and Luka. They're the amazing minds behind No-Fear Beer."

"Nice to meet you. I think I read in the news that you sold your business a few years ago for quite a chunk of change," Mike said.

"Yep, and then they ruined it. They changed the quality of a key ingredient, and it's nothing like it used to be. So now that we're out of our non-compete clause, we've created a new beer," Nikola replied. "We spent ten years creating the perfect-tasting beer, launched it from our garage, and turned it into a business selling over five-million gallons a year. Within two years, they destroyed it. Unbelievable."

"Gee, that's terrible! I had no idea," Mike replied, feeling like his small questions had triggered a far more emotional response than he'd anticipated.

"Yeah. Luka thought it was the right thing to do, but he was wrong," griped Nikola.

The men burst into a fiery argument in their native tongue. Mike wasn't sure what Eastern European language they were fighting in. Vance just laughed.

"Hey, Mike, enjoy some food," he said, pointing to a dozen different dishes laid out on the table. "Look at what Suzi's prepared."

Mike gazed across the table at a huge platter of sushi. He had no idea where to start. It all looked amazing, so he piled up a plate and dug in.

"Wow, this sushi is amazing!" Mike exclaimed through a mouthful.

"Yes, it is. So, tell me what happened with your friends? It didn't look like it was as bad as you thought. I saw you laughing and ordering a round of drinks, so I guess it worked out," Vance said.

"Yes, it did. I can't believe I waited twenty years to reconnect with them. They've invited me to watch them play tomorrow night. I said I might go, but honestly, I have other responsibilities, like figuring out a way to get this money," Mike replied.

"So, do you guys want a beer?" Luka asked.

The brothers had stopped fighting, seemingly coming to some sort of truce.

"Yeah, sure," Vance replied. "Whatever you're having."

Mike shook his head. He had two unfinished beers in front of him, and he didn't have time to sit around getting drunk in the middle of the afternoon. He was here to learn from Vance and secretly wished the brothers would leave, so they could get back to it.

"Mike here is just starting to learn the superconscious process. Would you mind sharing with him what you believe is the secret of your success?" Vance asked Nikola as Luka left for the bar.

"Sure, other than the obvious of walking the path, what made our business successful is the product. I used to work for a big brewery that had been making mass-produced beer for decades, and we knew the product was shit. No flavour. So on the weekend, I was making my own microbrew, spending hours figuring out the perfect taste and flavour. When I finally got it right, I took it to the executive team at the brewery and had them taste it. They all agreed it was much better than theirs, but they decided not to invest in it. They said the market was oversaturated, and that even though my beer was good, it was too expensive to make. I knew they were wrong and that we had something great, so I convinced my brother to join me in starting the business with a small loan from our father. And the rest is history," Nikola said.

Luka made his way back to the table carrying four beers. Obviously overhearing the end of the account, he said, "Yeah, that's true, but it's only half the story. The reason why it was so successful was because of the sales and marketing I created. Many great-tasting products never succeed, because they don't have good marketing. To be the best beer in the world, people need to buy it. The brand and the story behind the brand are everything. I used to be in business development in the software industry. My task was building big relationships and selling computer systems to universities, Fortune 1000 companies, and governments. They were big, multi-billion-dollar deals, so coming into the beverage industry was easy. We took the market apart."

"But we wouldn't have been able to do it without the right product," Nikola added.

"You could have given me any beer, and I would have made it a success. I can sell anything," Luka shot back.

The sibling rivalry was fierce, but they were obviously a great team.

"Oh, would you two stop it," Vance interrupted. "Cheers to your success. It wouldn't have happened any other way. Selling a business for hundreds of millions is a big victory, and I'm so proud of you."

"We couldn't have done it without your mentorship and understanding the superconscious path," said Luka.

"Yeah, that's right," Nikola said. "Mike, what you won't read in all the press is that I had the product for over a year before I summoned up the courage to launch it. I knew I had a great product, but I didn't know anything about sales and marketing, so I was stuck. When I met Vance, he taught me a process that used intuition to figure out my next action, which annoyingly was to reach out to my brother for help. This was the last thing I wanted to do, but it was the best decision I made."

"See, I told you," Luka said, not wanting to miss an opportunity to get one up on his brother. "What we learned is that we needed to hold our focus on the end result and take intuitive action in spite of any perceived negative feelings. Even if the action is to ask your arrogant little brother to help you," Nikola said with a smile.

"I didn't want to work with you, either," Luka replied. "Actually, Mike, I was looking for an opportunity to apply my skills. After years of building other people's businesses, I decided I should have one of my own. And just like my older brother here, the last thing I wanted to do was work with him."

"Sounds like a match made in heaven," Mike said, laughing.

"Well, there's probably some truth in that. When more than one person is connected to the same end result, the magic is intensified, especially if they have complementary superpowers," said Vance.

"Yes, that's right," said Luka. "What we found is that since we were both aligned on the end result and learning from Vance, creating this business was easy. So, Mike, what is it that you do? Is Vance helping you on a project?"

"Yes, kind of. I'm a psychologist, but my main challenge is that in a little over a week, I have to get a large sum of money together to support my grandmother that I currently don't have. Vance began my superconscious education this morning."

"This morning! Oh, wow. You're in for a journey." Luka grinned. "If I can share one thing, it's to know that you will get triggered by your unconscious wound. But the faster you can become aware of your structure and re-focus on what you really desire, the faster you can let your superconscious figure out how to make it happen. If you listen to what Vance has to share, it will all work out. It did for us."

"We'd better let you two get on with it then," Nikola said, motioning to his brother.

"Mike, it was a pleasure to briefly meet you. Once you understand and have applied the knowledge you learn from Vance, reach out to me. We love doing business with others who understand the superconscious creation process. Maybe there will be some great synergy." The brothers got up, grabbed their beers, and walked away.

Mike was relieved to get time back with Vance. He really wanted to know what his superpower was, and Vance didn't waste any time continuing the lesson.

"Those guys are amazing. They have the combined superpowers that create great synergy. Nikola has the first superpower of perfection and discernment that I talked about before. His superpower was created in childhood from a wound of feeling as though he was defective. Without accessing that superpower, he would never have created their amazing beer. When he was stuck in his unconscious wound, he was super critical of himself, his workplace, and the product they were creating. He'd been making beer for fifteen years, scared of going out on his own, because his number one fear is being seen as imperfect and failing. He never would have taken the leap if it wasn't for Luka, who has the third superpower."

"That was the Achiever, right?"

"Exactly. It's the power of promotion, influence, and performance and is formed from a wound of never feeling like they're enough. This person only feels whole when they're achieving success in the eyes of people they believe are important. They learn that being successful and achieving feats that others think is impressive, makes them impressive. Without achievement, they feel like nothing. They strive for recognition and to be seen as the best. They're great promoters and salespeople. That's also why he's so boastful. He still lives a little in his unconscious wound, with an agenda for his older brother to say he's the best," said Vance.

"So, how do I access my superpower?" Mike asked.

Vance didn't have time to reply as someone was yelling out to them from across the bar.

"Hey, Dunny! You have to come and sing with us!"

Mike looked up to see Big T standing at the end of the VIP booth, puffing from running and clearly excited.

The band were all looking down from the top floor, waving Mike over to the karaoke room.

"Come on, Mike. It will be like old times. I'm sure you can spare ten minutes," Trev said. "We have 'With or Without You' ready to go. Remember when we used to play it in the basement at Jake's house?"

Mike smiled, remembering the good old days. They had so much fun in that basement, playing music.

"That's not very punk rock," Vance mocked.

"Yeah, but it's a great song." Trev laughed. "C'mon, Dunno, we're all waiting for you!"

"Go on," Vance urged. "What do you have to lose? How great would it be to sing with your old buddies?"

Mike wasn't buying it. "I'm sorry, Trev, I would love to, but I have a really pressing issue with my nana, and I need to get some more information from Vance here."

Big T's enthusiasm dropped from his face.

Hoping Vance would back him up, Mike said, "Sorry, I haven't introduced you two. Vance, this is Trevor. He plays the drums for the Raging Crows."

"Vance, good to meet you. Everyone calls me Big T," Trev said.

Vance said, "Well, Big T, we'll be up in a few minutes. We just have a few more things to cover."

"Okay, see you up there!" Trev replied, turning to the band with a big thumbs up and a fist pump to signal his solo mission was successful.

Mike smiled at his old bandmate, relieved Vance had defused the situation and that he'd stretch the five minutes for as long as needed.

He turned to Vance to thank him, only to see him frowning. "What's wrong?"

"Mike, you need to stop denying your true nature. Being a creator is about living in your desired reality, you need to be it now. You're so convinced you can't have what you want, you deny any chance of it happening. You're either a creator or not!" Vance said with passion.

"What? You're joking, right? Now's not the time to go and sing karaoke with old friends. I gave up the money to learn from you, and we keep getting interrupted. I only have a few days to get this straightened out!" Mike said in frustration.

"Exactly. And what I'm telling you is that you must follow the superconscious path by staying in the creative structure and not focusing on your wound," Vance said. "Do you remember the choice you made earlier today? To play music and maybe join a band?" Vance asked.

"Sure," Mike replied.

"Then, only a short time later, you're presented with an opportunity to reconnect with the very bandmates you spent a lot of your formative years with, and sing with them. Can you not see this is a direct reflection of your choice?" Vance asked. "Mike, the way of being a creator is having a desire and then following through on what you're presented with. If you want a reality where unbelievable magic happens on a regular basis, you can't deny opportunities when they present themselves. You're either living the superconscious path or not. If you want to create tens of thousands of dollars in a week, then you must live the creative reality, and if part of that new reality is playing in a band, and you deny it, then you're denying your magic. You're killing your creative power!"

"I'm sorry, Vance. I hadn't thought of it that way. I guess I've been so focused on my problems, I can't see anything else."

"The superconscious path is never obvious to the self-conscious mind, but it's quite predictable if you follow the process I'm teaching you. Let me share a little story. A few years after I launched my restaurants, I was having a difficult time. We'd grown to five locations, and my management team were stretched to the limit, under pressure, and fighting. I was so stressed out, working eighteen hours a day and still not keeping up. During this time, I reached out to my grandfather for advice. He invited me to go on a two-week fly-fishing trip to Montana. I couldn't believe what I was hearing. Wasn't he listening? I had an urgent problem that needed solving, so I thought the only reasonable reaction was to decline his invitation. But he reminded me that one of my written objectives was about getting outdoors and spending more time with family. He told me that if I denied this opportunity, I was denying my creative power. I was so scared that if I went away, everything would collapse, but I had to be vulnerable and leave my company in the hands of a management team that was super dysfunctional and at each other's throats."

"I can't believe you were able to do that."

"Once again, it was proven to me that the superconscious works in ways the self-conscious mind can never understand. On the flight over, I sat next to a beautiful lady, and we talked for hours and hours. Within three months, we were engaged. We got married later that year and have been together ever since. While I was away, a manager resigned, and this turned out to be a big blessing. The business flourished. I had a great time with my grandfather, and because of that trip, I now have three kids and a bunch of grandchildren with my beautiful wife. I can't imagine how life would have been if I hadn't gone," Vance said, chuckling.

"That's an amazing story."

"I hope I painted a clear picture for you. All you can do right now is focus on how you want things to be, and then take the intuitive action. You have a few of them written down. Check it out."

Mike read what he'd written earlier.

I choose to have a happy and healthy family.

I choose to make shitloads of money.

I choose to play music and maybe join a band.

"I'm so glad I wrote these down. This just happened, and I'd already forgotten."

"Mike, if you really want to learn to be a creator and turn your life around, you must allow the magic of the superconscious to play its part. You can't just turn it on or off. If you hadn't written down the choice of playing music in a band, then your situation would be different. But you did. It's what you told your superconscious you wanted to create, and within an hour, your old band is inviting you to sing karaoke with them. If that isn't magic, I don't know what is."

"Okay, you're right," Mike admitted. "It will be fun, and I did choose it. But after a couple of songs, I really want to get back to learning from you. Okay?"

Vance nodded. "You have a deal."

Both men filled a plate with sushi rolls and made their way through the crowd to the karaoke room. On arrival, they were met with a tray of shots and handed a microphone.

"Cheers!" the group yelled, thrusting a shot in front of Mike, which he begrudgingly took.

The music started, and the first words of U2's famous song flashed on the screen.

CHAPTER SEVEN

THE UNCONSCIOUS AGENDA

M ike was having the time of his life. He had no idea how many songs they'd sung or what time it was, but he didn't care.

Vance left a while ago, and the drinks hadn't stopped.

Mike's phone vibrated in his pocket. He pulled it out and was instantly stressed. It was June, and worse, she'd been calling non-stop. Then he realized in horror it had been four hours since that first song, and he knew he probably had some explaining to do.

He walked out of the small karaoke room to get some quiet.

"Hey, honey," he said in his sweetest tone.

"Mike, where are you? Are you okay? You were supposed to pick up the kids. They were waiting in the office. The school called and said you hadn't shown up. I had to leave work to get them!"

"Shoot, I forgot. I'm so sorry," Mike said, slurring his words a little.

"Where are you? I thought you went to a business meeting with Vance Vanderhill? June sounded concerned, angry, and a little confused.

"Yeeeeah, I lost track of time. Are the kids okay?" Mike replied.

"They're not exactly happy. It's two days in a row they've had to wait with the principal after school. It's embarrassing. Where are you? It sounds loud."

"Vance took me to this amazing restaurant in the old industrial part of town. It's unbelievable! We had sushi, and then my old bandmates turned up. Can you believe that? Literally Trev, Bobby, and Jake walked through the door. They're here to perform tomorrow night. Vance told me that part of my training was to follow my heart, so when they asked me to join them in singing karaoke, I couldn't resist," Mike said excitedly.

"What do you mean, training? Wait, Mike, are you drunk?"

"Uhhh...no not really.... I've had a couple," Mike replied.

"Is Vance there? Did he explain how he'll be able to help us or what? I've been waiting all day to hear from you!"

"I think he left a few hours ago, but that's not important. June, the most amazing thing happened—"

"So, you're at a bar, drunk with your old bandmates, without the person who can help us? While forgetting to pick up your kids? It sounds like you're taking this very seriously," she said, sarcasm dripping from her voice.

Mike had nothing to say.

"Michael, you keep reassuring me that you'll find a way out of our financial mess. All I asked was for you to go talk with Vance, so we didn't have to risk losing our house. Instead, you get drunk with your friends. You're so selfish! I can't believe you'd be this disrespectful and irresponsible. You're just like my father!" June yelled and then hung up.

Mike was in disbelief. He decided to walk outside to call June back, but she beat him to it. Before he could say hello, June asked in an accusing tone, "Is Jacqueline Maycroft there?"

"Yes," he replied.

"That's all I needed to know. Don't bother coming home tonight," June said in an eerily calm voice before hanging up again.

June had always felt Mike loved Jax and worried that one day he would leave her and run back to Jax. Mike tried calling back a few times, but the phone was switched off. He couldn't believe what happened. Here he was, out doing his best, and he still couldn't get it right.

He decided to head down to the bar and grab a glass of water. Sitting at the end of the bar, he felt hopeless, frustrated, and angry. His eyes teared up as he thought about how he was letting everyone down. He felt for the anxiety pills tucked in his pocket but decided against taking them, as they didn't go well with alcohol.

As he thought about the day, it became clear to him his situation was all Vance's fault. Vance had tricked him into not taking the money. It was his idea to have the drinks, and his idea for Mike to sing karaoke. He decided he needed to call Vance and set him straight.

The phone had hardly rung before Vance picked up.

"Mike, how's karaoke?" Vance answered in an upbeat tone.

Mike ignored the question. "Vance, you tricked me," Mike accused. "You said you would teach me how to create the money I need to help my nana, but instead all you've done is share some wacky ideas and tell me to go get drunk. Now you've left without finishing what you were teaching. I was supposed to pick up the kids from school, and June is mad. I can't believe you would do this to me. I came to you for help, and you just wasted my time!" Mike said angrily.

"Whoa, hold your horses," Vance replied. "This is your creation, not mine. I never told you to get drunk. I asked you what you really wanted to do. I shared that following your desire and taking the intuitive action is what a creator does. I thought we would stay for a few songs, but you kept on going. I was there for an hour and thoroughly enjoyed watching you all sing, but I had to be home. My family was expecting me," Vance replied. "What's really going on Mike? It seemed to me you were having a great time."

"Of course I was. I loved it. But like I told you, I have responsibilities. I can't be off partying like that," Mike shot back. "I told you this, but then you convinced me it was part of my training. I wish I'd just taken the money!" Mike blurted.

"Ah, there's the truth," Vance replied. "You do wish that. Right now, you're feeling powerless, frustrated, and wanting to make everyone happy. But the truth is, nothing is really wrong or changed from a few hours ago. Mike, this is your unconscious wound. It's found a way back to creating the experience of feeling powerless, needing to be saved, and worrying about losing your family. As I told you, the unconscious is so great at creating this experience, it will continue pulling you toward certain people and circumstances, to create the same result."

Mike calmed down, realizing Vance was right. He'd created all of this. Vance never told him to drink, and he did remember Vance asking him if he was ready to head back down to the restaurant after a few songs.

"So, Mike, what's the truth? Is it that you got caught up in the moment and forgot to pick up your kids? And is it also true that you enjoyed yourself? I'm sure your kids are fine and have likely made their way home and are safe. And June? She's probably mad, because her maternal instinct is to have her children looked after. I guess if she found out you were also drinking with old friends, it wouldn't have helped."

"That's exactly what happened. And since I'm with Jax, she feels threatened," Mike added.

"Yes, and that all seems like a normal reaction, doesn't it? You made some mistakes that I'm sure you'll learn from. All you need to do is go home, explain yourself, and apologize."

"Yes, but she said not to come home," Mike replied.

Vance laughed. "Oh, Mike, if I had a dollar for every time someone said something out of frustration that wasn't really what they wanted...well, I guess I'd be a billionaire." Then he got serious. "Mike, your unconscious has taken hold of you. It's creating a narrative to try and convince you that you're powerless, and you're about to lose your family. It's not reality. Literally none of it makes sense. Even when it comes to me leaving. When I told you I was going home, you were fine with it at the time, right?"

"Yeah," Mike said. "Sorry, Vance."

"No worries. I never take it personally. One thing I know is that everyone has an unconscious wound, including you...and your wife. So, how about you go home and straighten things out? Let's catch up tomorrow to continue your training."

"Sounds great, see you then," Mike said, before hanging up.

Mike was embarrassed for letting his temper get the best of him. And he felt even worse when he realized Vance must have taken care of the obviously substantial bill for their lunch that he'd been so worried about just a few hours ago.

He made his way upstairs to the karaoke room, where "Sweet Child of Mine" by Guns N Roses was in full swing. Mike joined in, linking arms and belting out the lyrics at top volume. Afterward, he bid farewell to his old friends, promising them he would see them at The Revolver the following night.

His car was still at the beach, and he was pretty tipsy, so he figured he'd take a walk. The cool, salty air would do him good. When he stepped outside, he found it was much colder than when he'd entered wearing only shorts and a T-shirt. It was going to be a cold walk, but he was up for it.

What a day! he thought to himself. It had been a roller coaster of emotions. Mike laughed to himself about how he'd turned down all of that money to learn the secrets of the superconscious creative process, the puppy eating the ice cream, and of course, connecting with Jake and the gang.

What a day," he repeated out loud.

As he walked, Mike realized he was starving. It had been hours since the sushi. He decided to go to the Fritz Point Fishery. It was Mike's favourite place as a kid. Pop used to bring him there on the nights his nan was out. It was their secret, as Nana would never allow junk food for dinner.

Walking inside, he instantly felt better. He made his way to the front and placed his order. All of that greasy food would surely soak up the alcohol.

"Hey, don't I know you?" a deep voice called out from one of the eat-in benches to the side of the small place. "Are you Dr. Dunne?" they asked.

Turning around, Mike saw a tall, skinny, African-American man, smiling at him. Mike did, in fact know this man. He was the father of one of his patients from his clinic. He was hard to forget because of the way he dressed, with his poorly tailored suits and tennis shoes. His hair was always messy, which matched his unkempt, greying beard.

"Hi, yes, how are you?" Mike asked, deliberately disguising any signs of his drinking. "You can call me Mike."

"I'm doing really well. You look cold dressed like that." The man laughed. "I'm Draymond. I don't think we've officially met. I'm—"

"You're Georgie's father," Mike said, making sure to sound like the doctor he was. "How's he doing? I haven't seen him in a few years."

"Actually, we're doing really great," Draymond answered. "The reason we took him to you is no longer a problem. It turns out, once I changed a few things and understood his unconscious orientation and wound, everything just worked itself out."

"Oh, really? By any chance, are you a friend of Vance Vanderhill?" Mike asked.

"He's my boss."

"Wow" Mike exclaimed. "I just spent the whole day with him!"

"What? You're kidding?" Draymond replied. "I manage his finances. Well, all of the family's money. I'm their chief investment officer."

"I can't believe it!"

"What have you been doing?"

"I reached out to him for some help with a financial challenge I'm having," Mike replied.

"Ah, I see. Has he started you on your conscious education?"

"Yep. We were just discussing superconscious superpowers, but we ran out of time."

"Life-changing information, isn't it? It's so great to understand the way you think you're broken or wounded is actually not a problem at all. It's the way we create our superpower. This knowledge changed everything for me," Draymond replied enthusiastically. "I have the fifth orientation wound, and superpower! Has Vance explained them all to you?"

"We started but didn't get that far into it, before we were interrupted."

"Ah, okay, well, take a seat," Draymond said, so Mike sat across from him. "The fifth orientation has the superpower of focus and intellect. I have the ability to be extremely curious about a niche subject and can devote hours and hours to it, learning to master every detail. This superpower is created from a wound of feeling unsafe in the world and retreating to my mind to try and figure everything out. To others, we can seem cold and not open to relationships. They might believe that nothing else matters as much as our work. We typically don't allow ourselves to be emotionally open or have a need to acquire nice things. All we really want is to be left alone and to work. Once I learned how to use my superpower and not get caught in the unconscious agenda, I was able to use it when needed, and also open up and connect with those I love. But I still don't want to have nice things," he said, laughing.

"It really is an awesome tool, and the results Vance has produced proves that it works," Mike said.

"Yes, it's great to understand yourself and know how to turn your desires into reality. Before, I was so frustrated with the world. I wondered what was wrong with me, as I was always criticized by others for being shut-down and cold. It led to my separation. I was always trying to fix myself. I went to countless therapy and healing sessions, which is what brought me to take Georgie to you. But the more I tried to fix it, the more stuck I felt. That is, until I met Vance and learned about the creative process."

Mike nodded. "Sounds familiar."

"Order seventy-two!" came a female voice.

"I think that's you," Draymond said, motioning to the ticket Mike was holding.

"Ah yes, it is." Mike grabbed his food from the counter and went back to his new friend, where he let his fish cool a bit before eating.

"As I was saying," Draymond said, "before I met Vance, I was stuck. Actually, back then, I was an economics and finance lecturer, and had multiple PhDs, yet I was making no money." He laughed. "Can you imagine that? Someone who lectures on finance was actually broke himself!?"

Mike shook his head. *It's like a psychologist who can't heal himself from his own fears.*

"I was so stuck in my unconscious wound, always feeling that I didn't know enough. But it just wasn't true. I had to let go of that idea and realize I knew more than anyone about the financial market and how to invest. With Vance's help, I started my own fund, and after a couple of years of amazing results, Vance became one of my biggest clients. With my intuition, letting go of the unconscious wound, and using the superconscious creative process, we're now the largest privately held fund in the state, with the best returns three years in a row. I still don't feel I know enough, but I'm getting there," he said thoughtfully, "It's my cross to bear."

"Wow, that's really incredible!" Mike exclaimed, realizing he'd now met another one of Vance's successful mentees.

"Yes, it is. When you learn the creative process and unleash your superpower, magic can happen. I've witnessed it with my own eyes. I've also seen many people not make it."

"Really?" Mike said, with a sinking feeling in his stomach.

"Since I manage Vance's money, many people he helps come to me. Some make it, some don't. Those who don't, always have the same story, or maybe different ones but with the same theme," said Draymond.

Mike felt worried he may fall into the group who wouldn't make it. He'd bet all of his success, not to mention a lot of rejected money, on Vance's teachings.

"What's their story?" Mike asked.

"They keep creating the same experience over and over again," Draymond replied. "Their unconscious doesn't feel safe trusting the superconscious, so they fall into the same patterns."

Draymond laughed as Mike ate a piping-hot french-fry and waved his hand in front of his mouth. After he swallowed, he said, "What do you mean by that?"

"When you follow the superconscious creation process, you're inspired to take action, even though it makes no sense. The unconscious doesn't trust things that are uncertain and don't make sense, so it creates feelings and thoughts that motivate you to not take the inspired action. But this is where the magic happens."

"I know all about the protection mechanism," Mike said testily, "with the unconscious wanting to keep everything the same as it's always been."

"Yes, that's right. I forgot, you're the psychologist." Draymond laughed. "Okay, let me give you an example. Just last week, I sold off assets for a client at a huge loss. A year ago, they got an offer from a competitor for sixty percent of their company. The offer was way more money than they ever needed, but their fear of being vulnerable and letting a competitor win, made them reject it. This was in opposition to the

action they were guided to take by the superconscious creation process. I mean, this guy is sixty-eight years old, and all he
really wanted to do was retire. Now, a year later, I'm selling
the company at half what he was offered," Draymond said,
shaking his head.

"Then why is he doing it?" Mike asked.

"Because he stopped following the superconscious path
and gave into his unconscious wound. You see, this same guy
got married three years ago and didn't get a prenup. He was
already a wealthy man, and we all advised him to get a pre-
nuptial agreement in place. But when his much-younger bride
refused to sign it and questioned his commitment and love, he
bowed out. Now they're getting a divorce. He has to make
quite a large payout and needs to sell this company. It unfortunately happens all the time," Draymond said.

Mike shook his head. "It's amazing how people on the outside can see when someone's making a huge mistake."

"Yep. I've seen it time and again. You need to be courageous enough to follow the inspired action in spite of your unconscious objection. When I left my position at the university,
everyone told me I was crazy, and I felt it. But I followed
through, and because of it, everything in my life is better. My
son and I get along really well, I'm back with my wife, no longer
taking medication, making great money, and most of all, I'm
happy!" Draymond said, as he got up from the bench. "Well,
it's been a pleasure chatting, Dr. Dunne. Sorry I chewed your
ear off, but I must be going. Thank you so much for your help
with Georgie. Good luck with everything."

Draymond turned and left as Mike laughed to himself at
Draymond's abrupt ending and overshare of personal information. It was easy to spot Draymond's orientation. It was

exactly the same as all the characters on his favourite TV show *The Big Bang Theory.*

Well, that was a sobering conversation, Mike thought to himself as he finished off his food, which was finally at the correct eating temperature.

CHAPTER EIGHT

STOP THE SPIN

It was late when Mike got home. He opened the door quietly and made his way to the guest bedroom, knowing his wife well enough that trying to talk tonight would only make matters worse. So he got into bed and set the alarm for 6:45 a.m., early enough, so he could make everyone breakfast.

The next morning, Mike made his way into the kitchen and started on his famous pancakes. He knew the smell would be irresistible to his sleeping family, and he smiled as he remembered all the lessons from the previous day.

It occurred to him to visualize what he wanted to happen. He closed his eyes and pictured his family happily eating the food he'd prepared. His apology has been accepted, and his wife is smiling and laughing at herself for overreacting and being jealous. It was going to be a great morning.

He was wrong.

When Mike was nearly done, he yelled, "Who wants breakfast?"

No reply.

"Pancakes are ready... I'll eat them all myself!"

Silence.

Now he was suspicious. He checked both the kids' rooms. Empty. His heart racing, he opened the door to his own bedroom, but nobody was there.

Where was his family?

Mike picked up his phone and called June who said, "H'llo?" in a sleepy voice.

"Where are you?" Mike asked.

"We're at my parents' house. What time is it?"

"It's seven a.m., June. You didn't think to leave me a note?" Mike asked angrily.

"They invited us over for dinner, and we decided to stay over. I'm going back to sleep. Bye." June hung up.

Mike was furious. June hated going to her parents' house. They lived an hour away, and she didn't get along with her stepfather.

Here Mike was, doing everything he could, working super late hours, fighting for his family, and trying his best to figure everything out. And what did he get in return? Nothing! In fact, less than nothing. What he got was his wife choosing to run off without even letting him know they were okay. He'd never experienced this with his June, ever.

He sat down at the breakfast table by himself to eat the pancakes he'd lovingly made for his family. After a few bites, his phone rang.

"June?" Mike said, with a hopeful note in his voice.

"It's Vance. Don't you look at the phone before picking it up? It's not the nineties, man!" he said.

Mike was in no mood for jokes. "I didn't look, Vance, it's seven a.m. I was expecting my wife."

"No worries. Hey, I know it's early, but I was calling to organize our meeting today. Do you still want to do it? What time suits you?" Vance asked.

"Yes, of course. I have some work to do this morning for my real estate business. I'll be putting up some signs and dropping off flyers. I'm still hoping to land a big deal, so I can put all this behind me."

"Okay, so how about four p.m.?" Vance asked. "I'll pick you up. Just text me the address."

"Sounds good," Mike replied and hung up.

He texted the address to Vance and took a shower to wash away the booze and greasy food, not to mention the bad vibes. And it was only seven in the morning!

The day went by slowly for Mike. He kept waiting for his phone to ring, but it never did. At four p.m. he walked outside to see an amazing jet-black Lamborghini pulling up out front.

As he made his way around to the passenger side, Mike took in the beauty of the car. The doors opened vertically, so he had to get nearly horizontal to squeeze into the low-riding sports car. He was blown away by the machine.

"Wow, what a beautiful car!" Mike said loudly over the roaring twelve-cylinder engine.

"It sure is," Vance said. "It's such a pleasure to drive." He smiled "I'm taking you to the race track!" Vance yelled as he put his foot down on the accelerator and launched the car onto the busy street. "Have you ever driven one of these?"

Mike was too busy holding onto his guts to reply.

As they raced their way through town, Mike felt famous. Everywhere they went, people turned their heads to stare and take pictures.

"Makes you feel a little bit like a supermodel wearing a bikini, doesn't it?" Vance said,

"It sure does!" Mike yelled back.

As they got out of town and cruised the freeway, the car engine noise dropped, and they were able to hear each other.

"So, guess what? I ran into Draymond last night, another one of your success stories. He's doing great. We sat and talked for a while."

Vance laughed. "Ah, Draymond. One of these days I'll get him to buy some nice clothes." He turned and looked at Mike. "So, what's the story with June?"

"Not sure. She took the kids and stayed at her parents' place last night. I don't know what to think."

"Sounds intense," Vance said solemnly. "All I know is that structure creates our reality, so we need to keep our focus on the end result. When we become more powerful and start following our truth, it can shift the relationship dynamic with people who are close to us. It's something I see often with those I help. It will all work out. She may just need some space. I guess it's been a hard few months for her, too?"

"More like a hard few years. June has been so supportive, but I think she's reached the breaking point. Actually, I know she has. I already told you how she pushed me into calling you. It was right after I pitched her on the idea of getting a second loan on the house. It's the first time I'd seen her upset at me in years," Mike replied.

"Why wouldn't she allow you to get the loan?" Vance asked.

"She's scared of taking on more debt and probably doubts that I can pay it back. And due to recent circumstances, I can certainly understand her feeling that way. But it's also because her father took on a lot of debt when she was young and went bankrupt. He spent the rest of her childhood working multiple jobs trying to pay it all back. He was never around, so June basically raised herself and her eight siblings."

"Wow, you don't hear about families that big these days," Vance said.

"Her parents were raised in large families, and they both loved it. There was always someone to play with and help out. So they decided to have a large brood of their own. But when her family fell on hard times, more responsibility fell on June, with her being the eldest. There were tough times without much money, and I know her worst fear is being that broke again."

Vance nodded. "That's understandable."

"She's an amazing woman, and I love her very much. But her reaction is completely unreasonable, especially since I'm trying so hard to get us out of this mess. We literally never fight, which makes this even worse."

The conversation fell silent for a while, but after a few moments, Vance said, "Mike, this might sound brutal, but I need to tell it to you straight."

"Okay."

"As I told you, the unconscious likes to repeat what we survived in the past. June is creating her experience of her father in you. Someone who makes bad business decisions and is never around for the family."

Mike didn't trust himself to speak, instead staring out the window.

"You can get as mad at me as you want, but I'm sorry, it's true. She's found herself a workaholic who's about to take on more debt he can't handle and would have to keep working to pay it off, while she's at home raising a family." After pausing to let this information sink in, Vance said, "If you take a step back and look at it objectively, I'm sure you'll be able to see it."

Mike was too choked up to reply. He could see the similarity, for sure. As a psychologist, it was easy to understand that his wife's overreaction was totally in line with what she'd experienced growing up. This realization made him feel more alone and helpless than ever before.

After a few minutes, Vance asked in a soft tone, "Are you okay, Mike? I know it's a lot to take in."

Mike nodded. "Yeah...I just..." He shook his head, still unable to speak.

"Living the superconscious path isn't for everyone. Learning to hold focus on what we desire, even when things seem to be going against us, is tough. I need to know if you want to continue. If this isn't for you, I understand."

Mike looked at Vance and saw he meant it.

"And I'll tell you what..."

They were stopped at a red light. Vance pulled out his wallet and retrieved the check he'd offered Mike just the day before. Then he handed it to Mike, who stared at it with uneasy excitement, knowing that he could be saved once again.

"Before you make your decision. How about you spend today with me at no risk? Keep the check in your pocket, and if at the end of the day you want to keep it, it's yours, no questions asked. But I want to remind you that by choosing to take the check, it will mean being saved, which is not what you really want."

"I understand," Mike said.

"From what you've told me about your wife, I believe she has the sixth superpower of safety. It's birthed out of a wound that the world is unsafe. These people can always sense a liar or an unsafe experience well before the rest of us. They look for someone to trust and believe in. If your beliefs coincide, they're a loyal ally, but if not, they can seem like the biggest rebels on the planet. They love to follow a strong leader and make great police officers, soldiers, and freedom fighters."

Mike laughed at this description. "That fits June perfectly. She's certain in her religious beliefs and in her youth was the first to picket and protest. I've never doubted her loyalty, and I've always cherished having someone like her in my life."

"Remember, each superpower has amazing abilities, but also a dark side, which is dysfunctional," Vance said. "The key to unlocking your superpower is to realize you're a superconscious creative energy that's immensely intuitive and genius. The problem is that in our society, we don't have an initiation process to reconnect us to our power and leave the childish wound behind, so, most people only experience the wounded side of their orientation."

"Yeah, I see it all the time. Many of my patients are stuck at the age of ten."

"Then you're well aware that no one escapes this wounding experience. But there comes a time when we must let them go. Most people don't. They believe they *are* the wounding and unfortunately never realize their full capacity. The way to rise out of it is to return to innocence," Vance said, as he pulled into the racetrack parking lot.

"Wait, what? Return to innocence? What do you mean?" Mike asked.

"We'll talk about it later," Vance said. "Right now, we get to have some fun."

The racetrack was packed, it was five p.m. on a Saturday. There were cars and people everywhere. As they drove in, all heads turned to see the black Lamborghini in all its glory.

Vance drove right past all the cars and parked in a bay, where the sign *Vanderhill Race Team* was proudly on display.

As they made their way over to the garage, Vance said, "Mike, I'd like you to get the most out of this. I promise that what you learn here will unlock your superconscious creative power and change your life forever. Your instructor is a special person I've known for a long time."

"Okay, I'm intrigued," Mike said.

"Dad, we've been waiting for you!" A tall, lanky woman in her twenties, with shoulder-length brown hair and twinkling brown eyes approached them. She had a natural beauty that seemed to emanate from her. "How are you?" she said, giving Vance a big hug.

"I'm great. Let's get Mike here set up for a drive." He turned to Mike and said, "I'd like you to meet my daughter, Allie. She'll get you set up."

"Nice to meet you, Mike, follow me to the locker room," said Allie.

Mike smiled and followed along, the lifesaving check still firmly jammed into the top pocket of his Levi's.

He put the tracksuit over his jeans, found a pair of boots that fit, and grabbed some gloves and a helmet. Each item of clothing had the initials VR on them, he assumed for Vanderhill Racing, or maybe it meant Very Rich? Mike laughed to himself. He was so excited to race that amazing car. And since he still hadn't heard from his wife, this would be a welcome distraction.

Mike headed out of the changing rooms, where Allie was there to greet him.

"You look the part," she said. "I'm going to be your instructor today. But first, I need you to sign a few forms. They basically say that this is dangerous, and we take no responsibility if you die," Allie said, laughing.

"Well, that may solve some of my problems. I have good insurance," Mike joked.

"If you follow what I say, you won't be needing any of that! But seriously, how much is the insurance?" she joked back.

Mike signed the paperwork and handed his life away to Allie.

"This is what we're going to be driving today," Allie said, pointing to a yellow Lotus race car.

Mike was deflated. "Not the Lamborghini?" he asked.

"Not on your first drive. Let's see how you handle this car first. It has a lot more power than you think. It's our training car and has a few special features," Allie said with a grin. "Jump into the passenger seat, and I'll get us started."

Mike got in grudgingly and buckled himself in before they made their way out onto the track. The small car was a tight fit. Sitting in the passenger seat, he was surprised to see there were pedals at his feet.

They made their way out onto the track, past the Lamborghini and a smiling, waving Vance. It had started to drizzle, and they maybe had an hour or so left of daylight. He reminded himself that this was a freebie, so he could just have fun driving some fast cars before going home and cashing his check. Then he'd find a way to pay Vance back. That would be the best for everyone involved.

"I'll take us on the first few laps to show you what this car can do!" Allie yelled to Mike.

Out of the pit lane they went, carefully building up speed, until they hit the open track.

"You ready?" Allie asked.

Mike nodded, and she floored it.

"Fuuuuuuuuuuuuck!" Mike yelled, when the car launched into full speed. He gripped onto the seatbelt as they flew around every corner and glanced at the speedometer to see they were going 165 mph. She didn't slow down until right before the corner, jamming on the brakes and turning hard. The car started skidding out toward the barrier, but Allie didn't flinch, while Mike braced himself for impact. Then, right before they hit the gravel, mere inches from the barrier, Allie drove out of the corner with precision.

After three laps of this, Allie rolled them back into the pit lane.

"How was that?" she asked.

"Terrifying," Mike joked. "I was sure you were going to hit the barrier a few times there. That was incredible! I'm still shaking," he said, holding his arms out as proof.

"Yeah, not a bad time," she said, pointing up to the digital timer, which showed the fastest lap time of two minutes and four seconds.

"Now it's your turn. You gonna beat my time?" Allie asked.

"There's no way I can do that," he replied. "I've got two kids at home!"

"What's that got to do with anything? Just kidding. It's not dangerous. Within an hour, I'll have you driving like a pro!" Allie replied.

"I'll give it my best shot, but seriously, you're an incredible driver. I think I'll take it quite a bit slower," Mike said.

"Mike, I *was* going slow. I'll totally have you going faster than that. I've never failed to get someone under two minutes," she said confidently.

"Well, I'm not ashamed to say I'll be the first."

"Don't talk yourself out of it! You want to learn how to be a creator, don't you?" Allie asked. "My father teaches so many people how to become superconscious and turn their biggest desires into reality. You either go for it, or you don't. What have you got to lose?"

"Oh, yeah," Mike said with a roll of his eyes, "what have I got to lose??"

Allie got out, and as Mike went over to the driver's side, he noticed the rain was getting heavier.

Allie was talking to her father, and they'd turned on the red light. All the other cars made their way off the track, so Mike assumed this meant it was unsafe to race and prepared himself to be let off the hook.

But then Allie walked over, jumped into the passenger seat, and gave Mike a big smile.

"Are you ready?" she asked him.

"Oh, I thought..."

"Yeah. I guess you saw them clearing the track. No, you're not off the hook," she said, laughing. "The key to racing is knowing what to do when you go into a spin, so we've taken all the other cars off the track, to make it safer for everyone. For your first few laps, I'll let you get used to the car, and then we'll start your training. Drive over to that mechanic, please," she said, pointing thirty feet ahead of them.

Mike drove over. The mechanic leaned into the passenger window, unscrewed a panel on the dashboard, and inserted a steering wheel in front of Allie.

"This is like training wheels on a bicycle," Allie said with enthusiasm.

Mike's face fell. He'd been driving cars for almost as long as she'd been alive. "Ouch."

"Okay, bad analogy. But if you know anything about driver training cars, you'd know that the instructor has controls on the passenger side, in case the student is about to drive off a cliff or something. It's just an added security measure, so we don't wind up crushed into the wall."

"I get it. You want me to get home to my family."

Allie laughed. "Yep. Okay, see this button here?" she said pointing to the middle of her steering wheel. "It will cause you to lose traction. I'll be pressing it at random times during your laps. If you're going around a corner, it will cause you to slide, and especially at the speed you'll be going, along with the wet ground, it's likely to turn into a full spin. This is so you can practice getting out of one. It's an essential skill for racing. When you feel the spin, it's important to set your focus on where you want to go, but if you're at the right speed, you won't need much acceleration to get out of it."

"Got it. I think. But it sounds a little scary not knowing when you'll press it."

Allie smiled. "You'll do fine. I haven't lost anyone yet!"

She gave her steering wheel a couple of turns, so he did as well.

Mike took a deep breath. "Okay, I'm ready!"

"Great! Go into the pit lane and then onto the track."

With no other cars there, Mike was free to go at whatever speed he chose. He took his time getting used to the car, and then put his foot down.

Allie said, "Okay, now you've probably seen all the racing movies, so I'm sure you know to brake before the corner, and then accelerate out of it."

After a lap, he started getting the hang of it and really pushed it. Foot down on the back straight, he even let out an "Ooooh yeah!" and grinned as he perfected winding his way through a few corners. He was loving it.

Coming into his third lap, he decided to really go for it as he hit the first corner, and then BAM! His back wheels slid out from under him, and he was heading for the wall. All of a sudden, he noticed the wheel turn and the accelerator pedal go down slightly. Allie had taken over control of the vehicle. They made it out of the corner and just missed the wall.

As they came to a stop, Mike's heart was pounding. "Allie, that was close! Did you press the button? How about some warning next time?" Mike said, still shaking.

Allie gave him a knowing grin. "There are no warnings in life. This is how you learn. Remember what I said about focusing on where you want to go and steering toward it? What you just did nearly killed us. As soon as you started spinning, you looked right at the wall, in essence, what you didn't want. Next time, concentrate on where you want to go. Don't worry. I'll be here, and I don't intend on dying today." She fixed him with a determined look. "Don't let this psych you out. Get right back to it. You got this. Go! Go!"

Mike did as he was told. He started out tentatively, going around corners at seventy-eighty percent full speed. Heading through an S bend, he felt the wheels start to slide, but he was determined. He turned to where he wanted to go and put his foot down, but the car started spinning even more. He was heading for the wall, when he jammed on the brakes and skidded across the gravel, coming to a stop about three feet away.

"What happened? I did what you said. I looked at where we were going and went for it," Mike said with a confused look.

"Yes, but since you had the car going so slow to begin with, the acceleration caused the spin to increase. You can't play half hearted, Mike. You need to have the car moving at full speed, so when you accelerate, the difference between your current speed and acceleration is minimized." She sighed. "In case you haven't guessed, my dad didn't just take you here for a day of fun. Everything you're learning directly relates to his teachings. If you use this example, you could be cruising along in life, when your world is sent into a tailspin, so you suddenly have to make a massive course correction to change it and wind up in a dangerous situation."

"I get it. If I'm trying to solve my problems without really knowing where I'm going or how to get there, I end up like I am now, having to scramble to figure out a plan before it's too late, and I hit that wall."

"Right. Now try it again."

Mike started out on the track again and spent the next ten minutes totally frustrated, nearly hitting the wall multiple times.

"You need to trust yourself, Mike!" Allie yelled. "This lap, I want you to set your best time. Let's go for it!"

"Okay!" Mike yelled back. He floored the accelerator and sprinted down the back straight, reaching a speed of over 150 mph. Coming up to the first turn, he felt anxious and started backing off. Going into the corner on the wrong line, he felt the car start to slide.

Allie reached over with one hand and pushed his head to focus in the correct direction. "Turn!" she yelled. "Push your foot into the accelerator! Now!"

Mike followed her instructions. He felt the car respond and pull itself through the corner, barely missing the wall. They stopped. Allie shut off the engine and turned to Mike.

"Well done," she said. "Mike, can I ask you a personal question?"

He nodded. "Sure."

"You're being tentative on the track. You seem so worried about me pressing the button, that you're not having much fun. Can you see how it might relate to your life?"

"What do you mean?"

Do you ease up when you think something is difficult, so you don't get overwhelmed and fail? Do you worry about problems ahead of time, even when they haven't happened yet? In times of stress, do you focus on the worst-case scenario? Do you lack self-trust and confidence to find a way out of any problem? Are you so scared of failing, you rule out any possible chance of success?"

Mike was silent for a moment. She'd nailed it.

"Do you want to be someone who takes charge? Who comes out on top no matter what? Who plays life full-out? Has fun and creates what they desire? Do you want to be like that, Mike?"

"Of course," Mike replied, feeling insulted that this young woman would insinuate he wasn't already like that.

"Well, effen show me, then!"

Mike felt the blood rush to his face. He was embarrassed that she'd described him so perfectly. He knew he had it in him. He'd show her.

"I'm going to beat your time!" he said, trying to regain some of his pride.

"A thousand dollars says you can't," Allie said, holding out her hand to shake on the deal. "My father said you've just acquired a large sum of money. So, let's go. Put your money where your mouth is."

"You have yourself a deal," Mike said without thinking. He grabbed her hand and shook. "But you won't press the button, will you?" he asked, suddenly worried he'd made a terrible mistake.

"Of course I'm going to press it, now let's go. I can't wait to take your money," she said, laughing.

Mike started up the engine and went for it. He didn't really care if he died. He was a little angry at Vance for telling Allie about the money, and at Allie for using it against him...but he wasn't going to back out. A fire burned inside of him. He'd win or die trying. At least he'd go out doing something fun and exciting.

Three corners in, the wheels started sliding. Mike locked his gaze forty-five degrees to the right, exactly where he wanted to go. The car kept skidding, but he didn't care. He stayed focused, waited for the car to turn around the apex, and then he floored it, racing out of the corner.

I'm going to win that money. Mike thought to himself as they crossed the starting line. They went around three more laps. Every time Allie pressed the traction control, Mike locked his gaze, focused on what he wanted, and the car followed. He was in total flow, and the car was reacting nicely.

After the third lap at breakneck speed, Mike started to relax. He knew exactly what to do and was no longer worried about Allie pressing the traction on or off. He roared around the laps, having no idea how fast he was going. Win or lose, he was doing his best.

Allie signalled to enter the pit lane. The racetrack light had turned green, and other cars were coming back onto the track. Mike drove into the garage, turned off the car, and took off his helmet.

"Wow!" Allie said as she took off her helmet. "That was amazing. Where did you learn to drive like that? You absolutely nailed it!"

Mike was having nothing of it. He knew he'd just lost a thousand bucks he didn't have. He couldn't think straight. It didn't feel like a victory, it felt like a war he'd barely survived.

As he got out of the car, he was confronted by Vance, who was grinning ear to ear, beaming with excitement.

"Mike, you just got the fastest lap by an amateur this year!" Vance yelled. "It's unbelievable! You did it in a training car, in the rain, and with Allie hitting the traction control on and off. What a drive!"

Mike couldn't hear anything Vance was saying. He was full of a fury he'd buried many years ago and couldn't take anything in. He made his way to the bathroom, where he splashed water on his face and stared at himself in the mirror. He didn't recognize the person looking back at him.

In that moment, Mike felt more power than he'd ever experienced before. He felt alive, dangerous, and ready for action. But he needed to ground himself back into his body. Just minutes ago, he hadn't cared if he lived or died. He'd driven like a maniac, clearly taking more risk than any other driver all year. He used the breathing techniques he taught others and was able to come back to some sense of normality. At last, he smiled at the man staring back at him. He'd shoved down this part of himself...the champion, a warrior, and a winner. He'd made this side of himself the villain. But in that moment, he realized this was the part of him that needed to be woken up if he was to turn his life around. He was buzzing with a new-found energy.

Mike made his way back out to the garage and went over to apologize to Allie.

"Sorry, I don't know what came over me," Mike said.

"Mike, don't apologize. That was amazing. I've never seen anyone drive like that. There wasn't a thing I could do to throw you off your game. You're a beast! Have you ever thought of taking up professional driving?"

"I don't think so. Beginner's luck I guess," Mike said, laughing. "There was no way I was going to let you take my money." He shook his head. "It was an incredible feeling. Once I stopped worrying about hitting the wall and kept my focus, I got nowhere near it, and it was easy," he said with a grin.

"You're kidding, right? Come look at this."

A crowd was gathered around the TV, watching Mike's race.

Mike realized in horror that as he'd skidded around multiple corners, barely missing the barrier a few times.

"Allie, I'm so sorry we were that close. This could have turned out really bad."

"No stress at all, Mike. When you're with someone who's that focused on where they're going, you're not scared at all. I could see you would get us through every corner. You were locked in."

Now that he knew he'd won the bet, he realized he wasn't the one who owed the money, it was Allie, but he didn't feel right taking it, after all she'd done for him. "Thanks. And Allie, don't worry about the money. I got much more than a thousand dollars' worth of learning from you today. I really want to thank you so much. I feel alive, and I get the lesson. There's nothing like having to actually face life or death to truly understand the power of focus. I was so fixated on where I was going, I didn't care if I hit the wall. I was all-in on the end result."

Allie smiled. "Hey, Mike, take the money. You won it fair and square," Allie said, handing him a stack of neatly folded hundred-dollar bills. "Well done. I hope your wife knows how lucky she is. You transformed into a super-focused, outcome-driven maniac on a mission. That level of power and focus is sexy!"

Mike blushed at being called sexy by this beautiful young woman.

POP! POP! POP!

Mike jumped, and then he was getting covered in liquid. He turned to find Vance and two of the guys from the garage holding bottles of champagne, celebrating by pouring it all over him. Mike realized it was too late to get out of the way, so he allowed the alcohol to cover him. Then he grabbed a bottle and took a big swig. It sure felt good to win.

He spent the next twenty minutes celebrating and talking with all the others from the track. Apparently, what he'd achieved that day was quite incredible.

Mike didn't get much time to celebrate. His phone vibrated in his pocket. It was Jake.

CHAPTER NINE

FOLLOW YOUR SUPERCONSCIOUS GUIDANCE

"Mike, it took me ages to get your phone number. For a real estate agent, you sure are hard to get a hold of! Anyway, we need you. Our bass player slipped and fell during rehearsal and broke his arm. He's okay, but he can't play tonight. Is there any chance you can fill in?"

"Ummmm, what?" Mike stalled, trying to take it all in.

"Dude, we need you," Jake said. "You can still play, right?"

"Yes, of course."

"Well, then, we could really use your help, and you don't even need to know the music. We'll have an iPad set up for you. It's okay if you can't. I know it's last-minute. I guess we can find someone else, but it would be fun to have the gang back together. What do you say?"

"I say yes!" Mike said with real confidence. After his win on the track, he was ready to take on the world. "Let's do it!"

"Great!" Jake replied. "Can you meet us at the Vanderhill Hotel? That's where we're staying."

"See you there," Mike replied.

"We have all the equipment you'll need. We start at around eleven p.m., but come down to the hotel as soon as you can, so we can get set up. Mike, thanks so much. This will be great! Just like old times. See you soon."

Mike hung up in disbelief. His choice of playing in a band was materializing in the perfect way. *This is unbelievable*, he thought to himself. *I'd better call and tell June.*

Mike was stunned and excited, but still full of courage. "Vance!" he called. "We need to head back to the city. I'm playing a gig tonight!"

Vance looked puzzled. "A gig?"

"Yeah, that was Jake. Their bass player broke his arm. They need me!" Mike was beaming.

"Magic!" Vance said with a smile. "Let's get going then."

They changed out of their wet tracksuits, said goodbye to Allie and her crew, and made their way over to the Lamborghini.

"Should I drive it back?" Mike joked.

"Not after what I just saw," Vance shot back. "You're crazy, man." As they made their way out, he said, "So, what did you learn from the racetrack?"

"Well, for one thing, your daughter is a great coach and driver. She really had me going out there. With Allie pressing the traction control button at random times while I was driving at over a hundred miles an hour in the rain, I felt like I was going to hit the wall for sure. But with her guidance, I stopped worrying and put my intention and focus on winning. Then something totally unexpected happened. I flipped a switch and gave up my fear of failure. It's strange to say this, but once that happened, I had nothing on my mind except where I wanted to go. I literally wasn't scared of dying. I didn't even realize how close I was to the wall, but it was incredible. It took a while to calm down. I'd almost forgotten I could feel that way. I can't believe it worked!"

"Yes, when you focus on what you want, you're in the creative structure, and you tap into the power of your superconscious to take genius-level actions. You kept your focus on where you wanted to go, not where you didn't. So, how does that apply to your life?" Vance asked.

"In my life I've been focusing on wall after wall after wall, and I keep hitting it. I don't need any metaphors to figure that one out!" Mike replied.

They both laughed.

"I want you to pay attention to what you just said. That you couldn't believe it worked. This is vital to your lessons. So many people live with the worldview that you must believe something will work to be successful, but it isn't true. If you only took action based on what you believed was possible, or in alignment with your beliefs, you would never have driven so amazingly well. You might not succeed the first time, but you will come out on top in the end. This is because of the learning feedback loop."

"What's that?"

"You start by being totally focused on the end result, take the required action, get feedback as to whether it works or not, create a new current reality with the new learning, and then refocus and take action based on this learning. Basically, you stay focused on what you really want and constantly adjust, until you achieve success."

"Got it," Mike replied. "But I'm betting it's easier said than done."

"Ha! You got that right." Then Vance patted his stomach. "You hungry?"

"Starving!" Mike replied

It had been a long day, and Mike hadn't eaten since his lonely pancake saga.

"Great, my golf club is just around the corner. I'll call ahead now," Vance said. "How do you like your steak? Medium rare?"

Mike nodded.

As Vance made the call, Mike slipped into his own thoughts. He desperately needed to speak to his wife. Was he really going to play punk rock with the Raging Crows? Had it been too long? Would he still know what to do?"

Looking out the small Lamborghini window, Mike noticed how dark it was for that time of day. Big, black clouds filled the whole sky, and the rain had gotten stronger. Up ahead of them, he could see three birds of prey eating a dead animal carcass on the side of the road and an eagle flying overhead. *Could that be an omen?*

Vance ended the call and said, "Mike, I want to finish our conversation from yesterday, if that's okay. I know this isn't the best place, but I think it's imperative that you understand all nine orientation points and their corresponding agendas and superpowers."

"Finally!" Mike blurted with excitement.

Vance laughed. "I love an eager student."

"I'm just looking forward to filling in the missing pieces."

"So, which are they?"

Mike looked at his notebook. "Four, eight, and nine."

"Okay. The fourth orientation point has the superpower of being able to understand and feel other people's emotions. Most artists, actors, and musicians have this power. It's formed out of a wound that they don't fit in or belong, and feeling like love was taken from them. This orientation creates total magic. Life would be so boring without this superpower. Have you ever noticed how art and music move us? This is because the people who have this superpower usually create all the art. They have the ability to intimately connect with the deepest human emotions. However, their unconscious wound is that they always feel like they're unloved, rejected, and don't fit in."

Mike nodded. "I see this with my friends in the band."

"Yes, that's right," Vance said. "This orientation would love the expression of punk rock, especially with how it can move people through emotion."

"You can say that again!"

"And finally, orientations eight and nine. The eighth orientational point has the superpower to lead, to be in charge, and be strong. This is born out of a wound where vulnerability was painful, and being strong was rewarded. They desire to be in control and never be seen as weak. This creates their superpower of knowing where people's power and strength lie. They love being a leader, standing up for others, and welcome any challenge."

"This is your orientation, isn't it?" Mike asked.

"Yes, I can definitely relate to this one. Also, the sixth orientation as well," Vance replied. "But when I'm really in my zone, I'm most happy fully immersed in understanding and learning, like the fifth orientation."

"Got it" Mike replied. "Sorry I interrupted. Please continue."

"That's fine, Mike. I always welcome questions. Anyway, the eighth superpower is mirrored with an unconscious wound that doesn't allow vulnerability, and this actually makes them weak. You see, an oak tree is strong, but when a tornado comes, it's ripped out. In comparison, a blade of grass is much more vulnerable, but when a tornado hits, it bends easily with the wind."

"Yes, got it," Mike replied."

"So, the last orientation is the ninth one. They have the superpower to heal, understand, and resolve conflict. This superpower gets overlooked, as the unconscious wound of this orientation is that they're a nobody. A person living in this orientation is most likely to have no goals in life and feel they aren't allowed to go for what they want. They never really decide who they're going to be. Usually, their only goals are about creating peace for others. The ninth superpower creates peacemakers, healers, and mediators. They have the ability to see all sides of a problem, because they feel like they have a little part of each superpower. It's quite remarkable. I like to say they have it all, the strength of eight, the sense of fun of seven, the dutifulness of six, the intellectualism of five, the creativity of four, the attractiveness of three, the generosity of two, the idealism of one, and the peace and flow of nine."

"Wow! Okay, I think I've got it. We all start out as a pure creative energy. Through our human journey, we encounter a loss of something we have a right to experience. This hurts and creates a wound, so we come up with a strategy to avoid feeling it again, which creates an intuitive superpower. So, if someone has the experience of feeling unloved, they could create a strategy of being needed and helping others in an attempt to earn and secure the love they think they've lost. Because of this strategy to be needed, an intuitive superpower of knowing what others need is formed. Do I have that right?" Mike asked.

"I couldn't have said it better myself," Vance replied.

"And since all our unconscious desires is to stay alive, it's always creating the same experience, because it knows it won't die from it. So, like with the second orientation, the person will continue creating ways to feel unloved and having to help others in order to win it," Mike said.

Vance nodded.

"This is why I'm always finding a way to feel that I'm about to lose my family and that I am powerless to change it. It's my unconscious recreating what it knows it can survive and is a direct reflection of what I experienced after losing my parents. It's the same for my wife. She created a husband willing to risk the family's finances on a business bet. Draymond would always find more things he had to learn before he was safe, and you would find battles you had to win. Holy crap! This is huge!" Mike said, thrilled to have it all coming together for him.

Vance just smiled. "Yes, we all have an unconscious wound, and if we give it power, we will always find a way to recreate the same experience, over and over again. But we can change our orientation and our life by refocusing our consciousness and creating a new structure. Just like you did on the racetrack when you stopped living in fear and focused on what you wanted. It allowed your superconscious to figure out how to drive like a professional and break all the records. We choose what we want, stay focused on it, and then let our superconscious figure out the rest."

"I just need to hold my focus, let go of everything else, and trust my superconscious to figure it out." After a few moments of silence, Mike asked, "So, how do I do that?"

"Do what?" Vance replied.

"Stop focusing on what I don't want to create? I can't go back in time and stop my parents from dying. And if I put all of my energy on healing the wound, then I'm back to looking at the wall."

"The best therapy on the planet is to build a life you love by living on the superconscious path. Shine a spotlight only on what you desire, and give up needing to know how it will work out. The only way you magically produced your results on the track was by staying in your end result. Did Allie tell you how to drive, or did she just get you focused on where to go?" Vance asked.

"She didn't tell me what to do at all."

"That's right, and you got amazing results. To live the superconscious path is to trust yourself. You're not broken, you're superconscious. You just forgot. You accessed your superconscious when you drove on the track. No one taught you to do that. But at over one-hundred-fifty miles per hour, you drove like a pro. You're a genius, Mike! Like we all are. Problem is, most of us never get to experience it, because we're so focused on the wall."

The big gates of Lakeview Golf Club swung open as they made their way down. There wasn't much light left in the day, but Mike could still make out the majestic links set on a beautiful countryside with views of a flowing river filling up a pristine lake. The club was members-only and off limits to the public, so Mike had only ever seen pictures of this place. He felt privileged and grateful as they drove in. And knowing the check was still safely tucked away in his pocket, he got a sense everything was going to turn out just right.

In that moment, Mike realized he hadn't thanked Vance. This generous billionaire owed him nothing but had taken time out of his busy life to help him. Man, he'd been such an ass!

"Vance, I just wanted to say how thankful I am for everything you're teaching me. I'm sorry I haven't been acting like

THE SUPERCONSCIOUS PATH • 143

myself. I've been under so much stress. You've gone out of your way to help me, and I've been critical, sarcastic, and rude. I'm sorry, and I really appreciate you."

Vance gave him a wry grin. "You've had your moments, but I understand that everyone has an unconscious wound, so I never take it personally. This may not be the case for others in your life. It might be a good idea to acknowledge and apologize to those who may not have the same understanding as I do."

Mike nodded. "I know exactly what you mean. Thank you for reminding me."

Driving through the parking lot, Mike saw so many luxurious cars. With a yearly membership in excess of what most people make in a year, this was the place for the big movers and shakers to meet and network.

Vance found a parking spot near the restaurant, sandwiched between a brand-new black Bentley and a vintage light-beige Mercedes. As they made their way over to the restaurant, Mike suddenly realized he was damp and sticky from the champagne, and his hair was a mess from wearing the helmet. He felt out of place and underdressed.

"I'll see you inside. I'm going to call June," he said.

"Sounds great," Vance replied, "but don't be too long. Our meals will be ready. Good luck."

He called his wife twice. June didn't pick up, which was unusual for her. She must be at her wit's end.

Mike thought about Vance's words as he reflected over the past year and realized just how awful he'd been. The irony of stressing out over looking after his family, while pushing them away because he was stressed out, wasn't lost on him. He decided to send her a text.

June, honey, I love you. I know I've been a real jerk. I'm with Vance, and I have the money thing covered. You were right. Everything is going to turn out ok. I'm sorry.

Then he figured he'd better come clean about tonight.

I'll be home late. Helping out my old band. Don't wait up. See you tomorrow.

Sending the texts did nothing to change how he was feeling. Should he call Jake and cancel? Then he shook his head and sighed. This was probably a question for Vance.

He walked into the golf club. When he caught his reflection in the mirror, he had to laugh. He looked like a homeless person, and that was exactly how the hostess treated him.

"May I help you?" she asked.

"Ah, yes, I'm here with Vance Vanderhill," Mike replied.

"Mr. Vanderhill?" the hostess said with raised eyebrows. "I haven't seen him today."

"He just walked in two minutes ago," Mike stated.

"I haven't seen him."

"Well, let me go in and find him. He just walked in," Mike said angrily, knowing he was being judged and feeling completely out of place.

"I can't let you do that. This is a members-only club. But I can assure you that Mr. Vanderhill hasn't been seated."

"I'm not lying. He just walked in," Mike said in frustration.

Just as Mike was about to launch into a full-blown argument Vance came out of the restroom and seemed surprised to see Mike standing there.

"Mike, that was fast. I only had time to shoot to the bathroom. Did June answer?"

Mike shook his head. "No, and that worries me."

"Mr. Vanderhill, great to see you," the hostess said. "Are you joining us for dinner tonight?"

"Yes, we are, Lilah. This is my guest, Dr. Michael Dunne. Sorry for our attire. We just left the racetrack, where Mike broke the amateur record!" he said, patting Mike on the back. I called in our order. We didn't get a table, so we'll be eating at the bar."

"Okay, sounds great. Right this way then," the hostess replied, before walking them through the doors and out onto the restaurant floor.

The place was packed, and it seemed all eyes were on them. Mike wasn't sure if it was because of his appearance or that the owner of the place was there, but everyone seemed to stop talking and look their way. Mike felt about two inches tall, judged and out of place. Here he was, unable to come up with money to keep his grandmother's care, in a room full of people who had cars worth twenty times the amount he needed.

Mike was relieved when they finally made their way up to the bar and sat down. Their meals were, in fact, ready, and came out fast. The huge steak was laid out on a wooden board with sides of mashed potatoes, broccolini, and mushrooms, all placed in small bowls to the left. On the right, was a tray of sauces.

Vance had already started dishing up the meal and was enthusiastically telling the bartender about Mike's conquest on the racetrack. It was all a bit much for Mike. He was literally sitting in an exclusive club, filled with the most successful people around, sharing a meal with one of the kindest, most generous, and richest men in his city. It really was magical.

"Thank you so much for bringing me here, Vance. This isn't something I get to experience. And to be surrounded by all of these successful people. It's totally out of my realm. There must be tens of billions of dollars in this room," Mike said, once the bartender walked away.

"Probably hundreds," Vance replied. "How does it make you feel?"

"Honestly, out of place," Mike replied. "I'm struggling to make ends meet, and everyone here is winning big. They're living the dream. They're successful, while I'm not. Plus, look at me. I'm not dressed for the occasion. I'm wet and dirty. I feel like I'm an imposter sitting here with you."

"Yes, I can tell. You're assuming you won't fit in," Vance replied. "When we drove in, you saw the cars. You know the history of this place, and you decided you wouldn't belong. You nearly picked a fight with the hostess, because you assumed she was judging you, and the whole time you've been here, your head is bowed, because you're trying not to be noticed or judged, am I right?"

"Is it that obvious?"

"It is," Vance replied. "So, right now, you're in a spin, your unconscious wound has taken your power, assuming that you will be rejected and you don't belong. You're looking at the wall, and you're about to hit it."

"What do you mean?"

"The wall of not belonging here. The wall of missed opportunity. The wall of not creating what you really want in the moment. Have you forgotten your other choices?"

"Of course not," Mike replied.

"Good, because I know you have a choice about making the money for your grandmother. Or have you given up on that and found comfort in my check saving you?"

The words stung, and he had to laugh. "It's hard to break old habits."

"Mike, there are likely ten to fifteen people here, if not more, who can help you create more money. They could teach you something, invest in an idea you have, or even assist you in dealing with your clinic's landlord. They may even have a property to sell. But all you're thinking about is the wall."

"You're probably right, but I'd embarrass myself approaching them looking like this," Mike said, pointing at his attire.

"You've hit the wall head on, without even trying to swerve," Vance said with passion. "Who cares what you're wearing? You have a story to tell! Isn't that what you wore to beat the amateur time on a wet racetrack, with Allie causing havoc? Did you ever stop to think that these people would be intrigued to talk to you about that? In a room full of designer brands and expensive haircuts, wouldn't you stand out? Why are you assuming you'll be rejected? I'm not saying you won't be, but you're giving up before it's even happened. You're not allowing a chance of success."

"I'll admit to feeling out of place, but I can't deny how I'm feeling."

"You have to come out of the spin!" Vance replied. "Remember, we have two different structures we can live in. The problem structure; where we're focused on the unconscious wound and taking action to avoid it, and the creative structure, that's focused on the outcome you want. Which one do you think you're in now? If this second, you shift into the creative structure and put your energy into a great result, you'll be able to activate your superconscious superpower. Everyone I teach is anxious to know what their superpower is, but the words aren't important. Committing to the end result is, because it allows your superconscious to access your superpower and come up with genius new ideas and ways to create what you desire." He looked at Mike for a moment and then said, "Let me show you. Close your eyes."

"Right now?"

"Yes, right now."

Mike closed his eyes.

"We first need to go to a place of innocence. Take a few breaths and remember what it was like before you decided how the world is, how you are, and what needs to be done. Connect with the innocence of a baby or a kitten playing with a leaf in the wind, or a child building sandcastles at the beach. Remember what it was like seeing things for the first time. Take a moment."

Mike remembered back to when his parents were still alive, and they would visit his grandparents. He remembered playing imaginary games and having fun for no reason. He remembered the first time he picked up a guitar and the joy of playing music. He reconnected with this part of himself, and it felt good. He smiled.

"Okay," Vance said. "Now define your end result by choosing it. Say in your mind what you would like to create."

Mike thought to himself, *I choose to have enough money to pay for all my bills and more. I'm looking after my nana, I have a happy wife and kids, and I'm going on vacation.* It felt so good. This is what he wanted.

"Got it," Mike said.

"Good," Vance said. "Now, in your mind's eye, notice where you are in this moment in comparison to these desires."

Mike thought about his day and that he was sitting here with Vance in the country club.

"I am."

"Okay. Now that you have the two points of the structure, the desired and current reality, what would be the best action you could take to move from where you are to where you want to go?" Vance asked.

Mike thought for a few moments, and then opened his eyes. "Vance, would you introduce me to people you think could help me make more money?"

"Yes!" Vance exclaimed. "I would love to. Right after we finish eating."

True to his world, after their bellies were full, Vance introduced Mike to a huge range of people, from bankers to property developers, artists, politicians, and celebrities. Every time Vance introduced Mike to a new person, it was as "Dr. Michael Dunne, the amateur race car champion and businessman." He made fun of how they were dressed, and the conversation flowed easily.

Mike was in deep conversation with an older couple, sharing how he won on the racetrack when Vance said, "Excuse me, but I need to remind you of the time." He then turned to the group and with a big smile added, "Other than being a record-holding race car driver, this man is a rock star playing to a sold-out crowd in a few hours. We'd better get going, Mike."

"Yes, you're right," Mike replied.

"Well, it sure was great meeting you, Michael," said a Hispanic woman, who was the president of a major tech corporation.

"Yes, we hope to meet up soon," added a well-dressed man in his forties, who was famous in the real estate world.

Mike and Vance made their way around, saying goodbye to everyone before heading for the exit.

It was now eight p.m. As they jumped back in the car, Mike patted himself on the back. He not only had an awesome time, he'd also made important connections with the who's who of Williamstown. He was beyond thrilled.

CHAPTER TEN

THE SECRET TO SUCCESS

Mike checked his phone to see a text message from June. It left him unsure where he stood with her.

Ok, sounds fun.

He didn't know what to make of that. Was she still pissed off at him? He figured her answering him was a good sign, but he wished she'd said more.

"So, did it work? Did you get rejected, or did you create magic?" Vance asked jokingly.

"Magic for sure," Mike replied.

"It was awesome to watch," Vance said. "Mike, what you just demonstrated is the secret to success. You have the ability to notice when you're giving the power to your unconscious wound and immediately switch to a creative structure. This won't be the last time you need to get out of a spin and refocus on what you really want, because your unconscious believes there are conditions that make it impossible for you to achieve it.

"I can see that. I keep stopping myself, thinking I don't deserve it or that people will judge me."

"Right. Whenever you go for something, your superconscious superpower gets overshadowed by your unconscious desire to keep things the same, creating a reality congruent with your unconscious wounding. Like when you decided you would be rejected, you looked for and found ways you didn't fit in."

Mike nodded. "And I did a good job of it, too. Until I let it go. It was like living in a different world where I was a powerful peer of the richest person in the state who fit in and was the life of the party. So if I understand what you're saying, I don't have to constantly think about what my superpower is, I just need to focus on what I want to create and trust it will guide me. By understanding each superpower and the wound I can easily tell if I am in the problem structure or in a creative structure?"

"Exactly!"

Mike sat in silence and processed this information. Then he said, "I have a question."

"Yes?"

"I'm not sure if I should go to the gig tonight. I want to smooth things over with June, but I know how much fun I'll have if I go and play. It's a once-in-a-lifetime opportunity. But I'm worried that if I go, it will just cause an even greater divide between me and my wife, and that's the last thing we need. It's been a stressful time for all of us. We've never had a big fight like this. I feel awful."

"Never?"

"No, never. We've had little disagreements, but nothing that's lasted longer than a day."

"I agree that sounds intense, but you must know it's normal. As a superconscious creator, you'll face internal conflict all the time. What I find helpful is drawing it out. It's easier to see it on paper than to just talk about it, so grab your notebook."

Mike pulled his notebook out and got his pen ready.

"Write CR on one side, and DR on the other, to represent your current and desired reality. Under 'current reality,' write 'having fight with wife' and 'invited to play with a band.'"

Mike did what he was told.

"Under 'desired reality,' write, 'happy wife and have fun playing with the band.'"

Mike added that to the drawing.

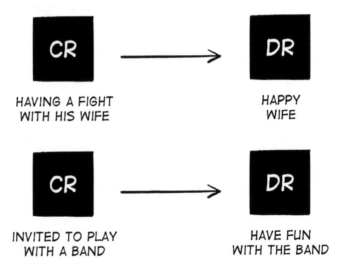

"Does this sum up the structure?" Vance asked.

"Yes," Mike replied.

"So, what's stopping you from having both? Why are they competing or in conflict?" Vance asked. "They don't seem mutually exclusive to me."

Mike stopped and thought for a second.

"Well normally, they wouldn't be. But we're having this big fight. I'm worried that playing tonight will cause our argument to blow up into something bigger. So, I guess it's fear," he replied. "Fear that if I go out, things will get even worse between us."

"Good, write that down," Vance instructed. "If you have an upset wife, what will happen?"

Mike thought about it. "As silly as it sounds, I'm afraid she'll leave me, and then I'll lose my family," he said.

"Okay, put that down as well." After a few moments, Vance said, "So, what action is motivated by that fear?"

"Going directly home now and making everything right with June," Mike replied.

"Exactly!" said Vance. "And if you do that, you'll miss the opportunity to play in the band. So, in your mind, you're in total conflict. I get it."

Mike drew the full structure out, so he could see it. On the left was 'Fear I will lose my marriage,' a sideways arrow with the words 'Go home now' above it in the middle, and to the right 'Keep marriage together.' Vance was right. It was good to draw it out. He could see the conflict, because the action to go out and the action to go home couldn't both exist at once.

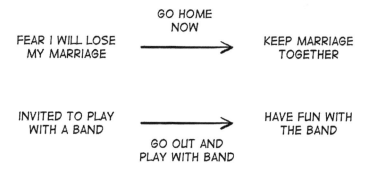

"Wow, look at that. No wonder I'm conflicted," he said without taking his eyes off his notebook.

"Yes, seeing it on paper allows you to be an observer of the structure." Vance paused and then said, "If you take action, you put the power in the fear, and you will always live from this orientation of having to lose something. The truth is, the unconscious is making decisions based on an event that happened years ago. It hasn't realized yet that upsetting your wife by playing in the band is nothing like what happened with your parents. Mike, will you really lose your wife and family by going out and enjoying a night with old friends? Is your relationship really that fragile?" Vance asked.

Mike had to think hard. "Even though it feels like it, I know it wouldn't happen. Our marriage is built on years of love and trust. Even the worst argument wouldn't cause that. Honestly, I'm just so scared, because I've never seen June this upset."

"That's true. It's likely the reason you've never had an argument this bad is because you always run back to make sure everyone is okay. You're scared of making people mad, because they may leave you."

A light bulb went off in Mike's head as he remembered a lost memory. "That's right!" he said. "On the night my parents died, I had a huge fight with my mother, because I wanted to go with them. I remember it clearly now."

"Sounds about right." Vance said. "You've likely repeated this pattern many times. How often have you denied yourself, trying to please others and avoid fights?"

"Too many," Mike replied, shaking his head.

"And has it worked?"

"No, not really. I have my grandmother's situation, two struggling businesses, and children I don't get enough time with. Most importantly, I have to take medication to stay happy. It's total bullshit," Mike said with emotion. "It hasn't worked at all."

"So, are you ready to start having what you really want?" Vance asked.

"Yes!" Mike replied. "I am."

"Okay!" Vance said excitedly. "Let's get clear on what you choose to accomplish. I like to call them choices and not goals, because a choice is something I've decided I will experience, not a wish. But before you answer, there are a few things you should know. They should be clear and stated in the positive, and they must be able to be completed by you alone, and no one else. For example, you can't have a choice to have a healthy and happy grandmother or wife or children. That's up to them. You can, however, choose to be the best father or husband or grandson you can be, and to help them in ways you believe are useful."

Mike nodded. "So, do you have any suggestions?"

"From talking to you over the past couple of days, here are the choices I would suggest. One is to make more than enough money to support your family, two is having a great marriage, number three is playing in a band and having a great time, and the fourth is to be a great father. Would you agree?"

"Yes," Mike replied.

"Great, now we're getting somewhere. Go ahead and write down the creative structure for each choice. You will remember that the creative structure is made up of two points, and an action to move towards what you desire. First comes the desired reality, which is what you want to create, invent, manifest, or experience. Second is the current reality, which is where you are in life compared to the desired reality. Third is the action to move you from where you are to where you want to be. Draw out the current reality and desired reality for each choice and leave space for us to fill in the action," Vance said.

Mike wrote:

DR: Making enough money to support family.
CR: Struggling in business. Have a $50k check. Learning from Vance.

DR: Having a great marriage.
CR: In a great marriage but having a fight. I've been distant and not communicating well.

DR: Playing in the band tonight.
CR: In the car on the way there, feeling uncertain.

DR: Being a great father.
CR:Not enough quality time with kids. Forgot to pick them up from school.

"Done," Mike said, before reading them aloud to Vance.

"Knowing the next action is crucial. The superconscious is like headlight beams. It will only share a little bit of what's in front of you," Vance said as he turned off the lights on the Lamborghini and left them off. The road went dark.

After about two seconds, Mike couldn't take anymore. "Turn the lights back on!" he yelled, totally freaked out.

Vance turned the lights on and laughed. "You have to trust that once you move forward, the next action is obvious, just like we're following the GPS to this hotel. We have no idea what's around the corner."

"Okay, got it. Just don't do that again," Mike said. "So, how do I decide on the next action when I have two that seem in conflict? I can't be playing in the band and at home with my wife."

"By using the superconscious creation process," Vance replied. "To do this, you must visualize the desired reality as completed and build a full sensory experience of it. In your image, you're looking back to the current reality and teaching yourself what your next action is. Remember, you know where you will end up, but you can only see a few feet in front of you. All you can do is forge ahead and trust the rest will happen as it should."

"Okay, I'll give it a go," Mike said, before closing his eyes and following instructions. It took some time, but after a few minutes, Mike opened his eyes and wrote an action under each choice.

DR: To make enough money to support family.

CR: Struggling in business. Have a $50k check. Learning from Vance.

Action: Take meetings with new connections from the golf club.

DR: To have a great marriage.

CR: In a great marriage but having a fight. I've been distant and not communicating well.

Action: Text June and suggest a date at the beach tomorrow.

DR - To play in the band tonight.

CR - In the car on the way there, feeling uncertain.

Action: Play with the band, have a great time.

DR - Be a great father.

CR - Not enough quality time, forgot to pick them up from school.

Action: Be present with them in the evenings, no distractions.

After writing it all out, he read each action aloud to Vance.

"Wow! You're getting it," Vance said. "That sounds like a great list of creations. But here's the secret: you must follow through. If you don't, it is because you're putting the power in your unconscious. This is why writing it out is so important. Creating is simple when you know what you're doing."

Mike pulled out his phone and took his first action, texting June.

Honey, I'm sorry. I know my actions may seem strange. I'm learning a lot from Vance. I love you. I'm so excited to play with my old band tonight. It's a dream come true. But tomorrow, let's have an afternoon at the beach, like we used to. I have a lot to share with you.

It felt good to state the truth. Mike felt relieved and sat in silence, reflecting on his new choices. The best therapy was to create a life he loved, and it felt good.

It took another twenty minutes to arrive at the hotel, and of course, since it was Vance's, they went in a VIP entrance and through the back.

"Mike, I have a suite here. You can have a shower and get changed," Vance said. "Allie and her husband have a room here as well, and he's about your size. You'll be able to grab some of his spare clothes. In fact, if you want to stay the night, you're welcome."

"Thanks!" Mike said, relieved. He really needed a shower.

Vance took Mike to the front desk to explain that he was a good friend of his and to give him access to a penthouse suite, as well as a key to Allie's room. Then he said, "Mike, last night you gave your power away to alcohol, you didn't really want to drink but you got swept up in the moment and then got angry at me. Remember you are powerful, you don't need those pills or alcohol to be confident. Have a great time tonight, if you choose to have a drink, do it consciously. Stay in your end result, and take the correct action. Everything will work out for you," Vance said with a smile.

"Got it. Thanks for everything, Vance," Mike replied.

Mike took the elevator to the penthouse. He found Allie's room, where he grabbed a pair of jeans and an old T-shirt, before heading over to his own room. It was breathtaking, with four-bedrooms, a bar, an infinity pool, and a view of the whole town out to the sea. Mike didn't have long to take it all in, though. He was running out of time.

It felt great stepping into the shower, warm water rinsing off the cold, sticky champagne. He felt excited. Tonight was going to be special, and tomorrow, he would open up to June. Then with the money from Vance, he would save his grandmother, and that's when the real work would start. He would find a way to pay Vance back, reconnect with his children, and create a life he loved. In just a few days, he felt like he'd been handed the keys to the Universe.

His peaceful shower was interrupted by his phone. Mike got out of the shower, hoping it was June. It was Jax.

"Mike, where are you? Are you still coming? The guys are on in a few hours!" Jax's voice was just barely audible over loud music and the noise of a party going on.

"Of course. I'm here in the hotel taking a shower. What room number are you in? I'll be there in a few."

"Sixth floor, room 33," Jax replied.

"See you there!" he said.

Mike got ready in a hurry and raced out the door. As he left, he glanced at his phone; it was a text from June.

Looking forward to it

Mike was pleased that June had replied. He was going to have a great time with her tomorrow. Everything was coming together perfectly. Now, he could just go and enjoy his night.

Stepping out of the elevator, Mike didn't need to guess what room the band was in, he could hear it. He knocked and was greeted by someone who took Mike by surprise. It was a tall, middle-aged man wearing skinny yellow jeans ripped at the knee, a leather jacket, and a white singlet stretched over his pregnant-looking belly. He had black eye makeup on and looked like he'd stepped out of a Sex Pistols concert from the 1980s.

Mike introduced himself and was ushered in. He soon realized everyone was dressed the same way. Somehow, he hadn't realized there would be a dress code. He instantly felt out of place and regretted being there.

But remembering his experience at the restaurant, he closed his eyes and visualized the end result. *I choose to have a great time playing with the band tonight.* Then he asked for intuitive guidance. After a few seconds, he opened his eyes and saw Jax over by the kitchen, talking with a few people.

He confidently walked over, tapped her on the shoulder, and asked, "Who's in charge of hair and makeup?"

Jax turned around.

"Mikey!! You made it" she shrieked, swinging her arms around his neck.

Her touch sent chills across his whole body. She looked amazing wearing a black tank top, tight jeans, and knee-high boots.

"It's going to be a great night!" Jax squealed.

"Dunny! You made it!" Bobby yelled from a nearby couch.

"Hey, Mike Shithouse. Thanks for finally turning up!" Jake added.

"I thought I smelled something horrible walk through the door!" Big T yelled from behind three women to his left.

Apparently, his friends were still not over the immature joke. After Jake's mom took a trip to Australia and told them that by adding a "y" to Mike's last name, it was the word they used for toilet, the guys never let him live it down.

"That smell is probably all the crap coming out of your mouth!" Mike yelled back. "Is that any way to talk to your saviour? I might just turn around and leave!" he said with a smile, faking walking toward the door. Then he turned around and said, "What? You weren't going to try and stop me?" He smiled. "I'm super excited to play with you guys, but I do have to admit, I may need to borrow some clothes, though," Mike said, pointing to himself. "When I left the house this morning, I didn't realize I was going to be playing with the famous Raging Crows. So, what do you say? Can you turn me into a punk rocker?"

"What about some of mine?" Trev asked.

"I can't wear anything of yours, you fat bastard." Mike replied.

Mike didn't know where this was coming from. He was confident and in control. As a reserved, respected doctor, this was way out of his normal comfort zone, but he just stayed in his end result of having a great night. He didn't focus on how he was with friends he once rejected and quit on, or the fact that he hadn't been in an environment like this since his teenage years. Plus, by fully dressing up, nobody in his "other world" would recognize him. It probably wouldn't bolster his reputation being seen performing with one of the most aggressive and notorious punk rock bands in the country.

Trev grabbed Mike a beer, and Bobby found some jeans. Jake came back with a studded leather jacket and a T-shirt that fit. Jax grabbed them and Mike's hand, and off they went to get ready.

Mike sat on the edge of the bed, with Jax down on two knees, intently focused on putting on his makeup. She had one hand on his thigh to balance herself and was only a few inches from his face. He hadn't been this intimately close with another woman in decades. He could smell her perfume and feel her breath against him. Plus, he couldn't help but look directly at her chest while having all sorts of inappropriate feelings. After all, this wasn't just anyone, this was his teenage girlfriend. His first love.

Mike was feeling out of control and needed to change his focus, he looked down at the un-touched beer Trev had given him. He chose to leave it untouched. Instead of taking a swig he chose to be powerful, he closed his eyes and refocused. "If you'd asked me two days ago if I'd be wearing makeup and going onstage to perform punk rock, I would have said you were dreaming."

"Hold still, will you?" Jax replied. "But yes, it's a huge surprise for all of us. We were so happy to run into you at Chow. And poor Jimmy. He's in the hospital. I hear his arm's broken in two places! But the guys are really excited to have you play, and so am I. It's a dream come true for all of us. We were all so shocked...you know, when you left."

"Yeah. We were just kids then. I had trouble communicating my feelings. I knew you would all be upset, so I kind of ran away. With Pop putting pressure on me to go to college, and then our breakup, I didn't know what to do. Leaving felt like the best option," Mike said, trying to hold back tears. "All I knew was that if I got a degree, I would have a stable income, a respectful job, and make my family proud."

Jax continued applying his makeup in silence.

"You know, I did come back one summer?" Mike said. "But you'd all moved on. There was someone new in the band, and you were in a relationship. It seemed there wasn't anything here for me."

"Yes, Mike, I knew you came back, and so did the guys. But we were all so angry at you. We felt betrayed, rejected, and abandoned. You really didn't make an effort to try, either" Jax said.

"I know why the guys would be angry, they didn't do anything. But why you? And why would I try to see someone who broke up with me?" Mike asked.

"I was furious with you!" Jax said. "You were the love of my teenage life. I cried myself to sleep when you didn't fight for our relationship. You just left."

Mike was silent.

"The only reason I broke up with you was that I read in a magazine that if a relationship was meant to be, you should break up and see if the guy will fight to have you back. Clearly, you didn't want me. I guess it worked out, though, didn't it? I have a great life and family, and so do you," Jax said with a smile.

"I guess so," Mike said, stunned by her admission.

"There, all finished!" Jax exclaimed. "Come look in the mirror."

Mike followed her into the bathroom and looked at this middle-aged man with big, black, star-shaped makeup around each eye. He laughed.

"Wow!" he yelled to her. "I hardly recognize myself." He pulled out his phone. "I better get a picture of it."

He took a selfie in the mirror before stripping down and putting on the ripped jeans, T-shirt, and leather jacket. That's when he realized in horror that he had no shoes to match the outfit, which meant putting on the old, damp tennies he'd been wearing all day. Then he folded up his clothes, and went back into the bedroom.

"What do ya think?" he asked Jax.

Jax burst out laughing and had to sit down on the bed. "You look perfect."

Mike laughed with her. He wasn't sure if she was amused by the doctor dressed in punk, the shoes, or just the whole situation, but the laughter felt good to ease the tension of the previous conversation.

Jake, Bobby, and Big T barged into the room.

"Ah, there you are! Here you go," Jake said, handing Mike a bass guitar and an iPad.

"On the tablet is everything you need to know. It has all of our music. We use it when we teach kids in our private lessons."

"I don't need it," Mike said.

Everyone stared at him in confusion.

"I'm actually your biggest fan. I've bought all of your albums for the last twenty years, and I know any and every song, especially your biggest hits, which I'm sure is mostly what we'll be playing."

"Really!?" Jake asked in shock.

"Okay, play 'Midnight Savage,'" Big T challenged him.

Mike loved this song. In fact, it was partly written by him and started off with a bass solo similar to "Another One Bites the Dust" by Queen.

"Okay, where's the amp?" Mike asked.

"We have a full setup in the next room. We'd planned a dress rehearsal," Jake said.

"What are you waiting for, then? Let's go!" Mike said with enthusiasm.

They made their way through to the spare room. Mike was nervous. This was the moment he'd thought about for years.

Mike plugged in his amp and got his bass set up and ready. They all put on headphones, so only they could hear the music.

Big T counted them in. Mike knew the song and what to do. After thirty seconds, Bobby joined in on guitar, and then Jake started the slow, rap-like beginning. Before long, the energy lifted, and they rocked out.

Jake turned to face Mike. So did Bobby. Big T was smiling, and the four friends reconnected in an unspoken way only musicians would understand. It was perfect.

The band didn't stop after one song. Half an hour passed like it was seconds.

"Wow, Mike, that was impressive," Jake said, taking off his headset. "You really do know all the songs. You're even better than I remember. We never really found anyone who gelled with us like you do. This is so fitting for our platinum anniversary tour."

Mike beamed with pride. "Thanks!"

They walked back into the other room to find the party had disappeared. Obviously, the guests had left to catch some of the warmup acts.

The band was ready. After picking up a couple of guitars and a bottle of vodka, they left everything else there. Mike wondered what was awaiting him.

It was a short walk to the venue, which gave Mike time to catch his breath and enjoy the moment. It was around 10:30 p.m. on a Saturday, and he was aware of just how outrageous the group looked all dressed in punk rock attire. He loved it.

They were playing at Revolver, which was the premier live music venue. It held up to 6,000 people with stadium-like, multi-layered terraced seating and a standing room bottom floor. It was awesome.

Walking with his friends, he felt a sense of pride as people recognized who they were. A guy leaned out a car window and yelled out to them, "Punk rock's not dead!" A few groups of three or four people joined in their walk, excitedly talking to the band members. Mike realized just how famous his friends were to these fans. It had been over ten years since they'd played live in their hometown. This was going to be bigger than Mike had thought.

As they got closer to the venue, they could hear the music from a few blocks away, and Mike started getting that performance anxiety feeling.

"Hey, guys, just how big do you think attendance is?"

"Sold out!" one of the groupies shouted.

Everyone had their game faces on. Big T was chatting to a couple of women, Jake was swigging from the vodka bottle, and Bobby was lighting a cigarette.

Mike could feel his stomach turning. He hadn't played in front of a crowd in decades.

"Are you feeling alright?" Jake asked, laughing.

Mike nodded. "Yeah, I think the reality is finally hitting me."

He was starting to wish he'd brought the iPad.

They got to the venue and made their way through to the green room. The noise was deafening. The two bands that played before them got the crowd fired up and ready. Because of encores and other delays, they weren't going to start until close to midnight. This was okay with Mike, as his nerves were starting to get to him. He needed some time to himself to calm down.

He walked to the side of the stage to peek out and see the crowd. The band before them was jumping around the stage with lights and smoke. The audience was going crazy.

What have I gotten myself into? Mike thought to himself. He was starting to panic.

To his right was the bathroom, so he snuck in and closed the door behind him. He went into a stall and quietly freaked out.

What was he doing here? This wasn't him! He was a clinical psychologist, father, and husband. He was just trying to save his family. This was ridiculous! How had he gotten himself into this mess?

After a few minutes, he decided he needed to tell Jake he couldn't do it. He would suggest that they run back to the hotel, grab the iPad, and ask one of the other bassists from the earlier bands to fill in. They would be fine. Most people in the industry knew how to play Raging Crows' songs. They were the biggest act of the punk rock era. Mike would go back to his normal life, and everything would be fine.

Mike had made up his mind. He flushed the toilet to pretend he wasn't just hiding, even though they probably couldn't hear it, and made his way out to wash his hands, when he was met with his image in the mirror. He couldn't stop staring. There he was, in all his punk rock gear, about to walk out on his dream. He saw a scared little boy, one who wanted to stay safe, who would rather run away and survive than go for what he loved and thrive.

Mike knew at that moment that if he left, if he let his unconscious fear get the better of him, he would never forgive himself. He knew that the way he was being in this moment was going to predict how he would be in all areas of his life. He couldn't leave. Even if he went out and failed, it would be better than quitting. He decided to remember his training.

He closed his eyes and decided to neutralize the wound. He thought of the worst-case scenario; that he would forget how to play and look like a fool. That he would be embarrassed and prove to himself, and everyone else, that he was a loser and not powerful. Then he decided to neutralize the negative thought by asking what good was in the bad. What would really happen?

After a minute, he realized that even if he did embarrass himself, it wouldn't really matter. No one would know. He was in full makeup. And the band? They'd understand, and he would just go back to life as normal.

Even if it all went horribly wrong, he would get some benefit by teaching himself he could be bigger than fear.

Then he remembered the next step, which was to visualize the desired reality, notice the current reality, and ask for the superconscious action. He chose the end result of having a great time and performing an awesome set with the band. After another minute of visualization, he asked for intuitive guidance for the next step, and it came.

He opened his eyes, and Jax was standing there.

"Were you meditating?" she asked.

"Um, kinda," Mike replied.

"It's a big moment for all of us," Jax said, pulling out a tissue to wipe some of Mike's makeup that had smudged. "The band is waiting for you. Are you ready?"

"As ready as I'll ever be," Mike replied.

Mike walked back out. "Guys, I think I might screw this up," he admitted. "I'm more nervous than I can handle."

"It would be weird if you weren't," Big T replied instantly.

"Mike, just focus on the audience having a great time," Bobby said. "That's what they're here for. They've already heard all our songs, so they don't need us to be perfect."

Trev said, "Yeah, you don't need to be perfect, bro. I'm sure I speak for the band when I say we're just so grateful to have this moment with you. Focus on the audience and rocking out with them! Let's have a shitload of fun, Dunny!"

The group was in sync.

It was time to go on.

CHAPTER ELEVEN

CREATING THROUGH CONFLICT

M ike walked out on the stage. It was pitch-black, and the audience couldn't see them. Mike laughed, thinking of the similarity to driving on the pitch-black road.

You can only see the next action.

After taking his place on the stage, he took a deep breath and closed his eyes. *I choose the end result of having a fun time and rocking out.*

Big T counted them in for "Midnight Savage." Then came the drumbeat, and Mike knew what to do. He started the riff intro. Bobby followed, and then when Jake sang the first few words, the audience went crazy, the lights came on with a bang, and they were away.

The next two hours were a blur. Mike screwed up a little on nearly every song but just laughed it off and got back on track. The crowd didn't care. At one point, he walked right to the front of the stage and was rocking out with Bobby. A few members of the audience got onstage, and Jake even tried to crowd surf before realizing he was probably too old for that. The music flowed, the drinks flowed, and Mike felt as high as he could imagine. This was a dream come true.

They got to the end, with Jake making his final tributes. "Shout out to Big Trevor on the drums!" The crowd went wild. "Bobby on guitar!" The crowd roared. "And our long-lost founding member on bass, Dr. Michael Duuuuuune!" The crowd cheered.

So much for staying anonymous, Mike thought to himself.

"But most of all, I want to thank you, our fans for a great night and all your support over the years. The after-party is upstairs. Let's have some fun till the sun comes up, Williamstown!" Jake yelled.

The crowd cheered. And with that, the show was over.

Mike felt amazing. Coming off stage, he was buzzing, and his ears were ringing. It was the happiest he'd ever felt. What a night!

"Holy crap that was incredible!" Mike yelled to Jake as they walked backstage, followed by Bobby. Trev trailed behind with four or five women in tow.

"It sure was, man! That solo performance you gave in the middle was amazing. Where did that come from?" Jake asked.

"Just something I've been working on," Mike said with a smirk. "Let's grab a drink."

"I wonder how great we could have been if you never left," Jake said.

Mike ignored the question and grabbed enough drinks for the whole group, who all toasted in his honour.

"To Dunny!" Jake yelled, raising his drink.

"To Dunny!" they all yelled.

"Cheers!" Mike yelled back as he raised his bottle.

Despite the coaching from Vance, Mike did feel like having a drink with his bandmates. He was proud he didn't use it or medication to numb his nerves before the performance. It felt good to be consciously choosing instead of giving his power away. He decided he would have a few beers and enjoy the moment even if he usually didn't drink this much. He was just having fun playing the part of a rockstar. Tomorrow, he'd go back to being a responsible doctor and family man.

"Guys, I have to say, this night meant so much to me. I've been your biggest fan from a distance, and my major regret in life was not sticking with you," Mike said in a sombre tone.

"But if you didn't leave, you wouldn't have that amazing family and wife who you love!" Jax yelled from one of the tables nearby.

"Yeah, Mike, no regrets," Jake added.

"No regrets," echoed the group.

"Yeah, you're right," Mike admitted. "I would absolutely love to do this again and find more time to spend together. I didn't know how much I missed this until now. But I must be leaving. I have a very important date tomorrow."

"Really? The night's just starting!" Trevor said.

Mike nodded and smiled. He knew his end result, to make things right with his wife. He'd achieved what he wanted here, and a boozy night wasn't part of what he desired.

"You all have a great night, we'll catch up soon," he said, shaking hands with his three friends and receiving a couple of parting hugs from people he hardly knew.

"I'd better come with you," Jax said. "You'll need someone to get you into the room to get your stuff."

"Nah, it's okay. I'll grab it all tomorrow. You stay here," Mike replied.

"It'll only take a few minutes," Jax said. "It's no problem." Before leaving, she said, "I'm going with Mike to the hotel to get his things. I'll see you soon, babe," she said, and then kissed Jake on the cheek.

"You know, I nearly didn't come tonight," Mike said to Jax once they'd made their way out and onto the street.

"Really? Why?"

"June and I are having a big fight. I have so much stress in my life right now. My business, my grandmother, and my family. But I really wanted to come and heal old wounds. I'm so glad I did."

"You were amazing," Jax said, giving Mike's arm a squeeze. "It was like going back in time to our teenage years. I used to love seeing you with that guitar. You always looked so sexy and intense on stage," she said.

Mike chuckled. This was the second time today he'd been described that way. "Really?"

"Yeah. Back when you performed, you were aggressive, and then when you came offstage, you were so sweet. You made me feel like nothing else mattered to you. I felt like your whole world, and you were my rock. It was such a contrast from the men in my family, who were always leaving," Jax said, referring to the half-dozen stepfathers she'd had growing up. "You have this way of knowing what someone needs. It made such a big difference for me," she said.

"Yeah, it's my superpower...and also my biggest downfall."

Jax had a confused look on her face. "What do you mean?"

"My whole life, I've been so scared of people rejecting me that I put their needs first. Any sign of rejection was terrifying, so I'd avoid it at all costs, including my happiness and health. Yet, because of this fear, I developed a superpower to know what others need," he said, and then paused to let his own words sink in. "This fear of being rejected is why when you dumped me, I just left and never talked to you again."

They walked in silence for a few minutes, until Jax broke it by saying what they were both thinking. "I guess we really screwed it up, didn't we? I wonder how things would've turned out if I didn't read that silly magazine."

"Who knows?" Mike said, putting an arm around her and giving her a little hug.

"Yeah, who knows…." she replied.

They were only a few minutes from the hotel and walked the rest of the way in silence, both lost in their own thoughts about a life path that could have been. Mike was torn. It sure was hard to not feel the pangs of regret, despite his love for his wife and kids.

They made their way into the hotel and up to the band's room, immersed in idle chit-chat the whole way, eventually deciding that Mike would get together with them all in a few weeks for a barbecue and a real catch-up.

Mike went into the bedroom to get changed and even tried scrubbing the makeup off his face but was having no luck.

"Jax?" he called out. "Can you come in here and help me? "I can't get this makeup off!"

Jax came in with some face wipes and carefully started removing the makeup.

Mike didn't know if it was because he'd had a few too many, but having his long-lost love inches away from his face, with her perfect smile, bright-blue eyes, and low-cut top was just too much to not share his emotions.

"You know, I never stopped loving you," Mike blurted.

Jax stopped, took a step back, and smiled. "Same," she replied.

Mike's stomach was doing backflips, and his mind was racing. He'd spent decades believing Jax hadn't wanted him. To be told she still loved him filled him with a sense of joy, relief, and excitement he hadn't felt for a very long time.

"You know," Jax said, inching closer and reaching out to stroke his hair. "It's only you and me here. No one would know..." and she leaned in to kiss him.

Mike pulled his face away.

"Jax, I can't, I'm sorry," he said, The blood pulsing through his whole body. "Maybe in another lifetime. But I love my wife. I'm sorry I said that. I've made a commitment to my wife and family, and even if they never found out, I would know."

Jax looked a little hurt. "You're right," she said, taking a breath. Then she handed him the face wipes and walked out.

Mike took a big breath and looked at himself in the mirror, realizing how close he'd come to ruining the beautiful life he'd created.

It only took a couple of minutes to wipe off the rest of the makeup, but when he went back into the room, Jax wasn't there. He threw his shirt on without buttoning it and raced out to find her. The ride down the elevator only took a few seconds, but it felt like an eternity. He ran out into the lobby, and what he saw made him stop dead in his tracks, as his heart skipped a beat.

Jax was crying and talking with June. He hadn't even known she was here.

Mike walked up to the two women, and from the look on June's face, she was upset.

"Jax says you tried to kiss her and take advantage of her!" June said in an accusing tone.

"What? June, c'mon. You know I'd never do that.".

"You're a married man, Mike. I don't know why you'd think what you did was okay," Jax said.

"What are you talking about, Jax?! Is this a joke? Three minutes ago, you were trying to kiss me, and now you're running down here to lie to my wife? What are you trying to do?"

"You said you always loved me and then you tried to take advantage of me!" Jax replied. "June, he tried to have sex with me!"

"Jax, this is serious. You need to tell the truth and stop this. It's not funny."

Jax crossed her arms over her chest.

"I'm not going to stand here and let you manipulate my wife. You need to leave right now."

"How dare you!" Jax said. "You can't boss me around!"

"Fine, then we're leaving, and you'd better not follow us."

Mike didn't wait for an answer. He took June gently by the arm and led her away to a quieter spot where there was a small bench. The minute they sat down, he said, "June, honey, she's lying."

"I don't know what to think," she said coldly. "I tried calling and texting you, asking if there was a way you could get me a ticket, but you never answered."

"I'm so sorry! I didn't check," he said. "We were kinda rushed."

Mike pulled his phone from his borrowed jeans and saw five missed calls and three text messages from June.

"You were incredible tonight," she said. And then she burst into tears. "You've shut me out for months. I've tried to offer help and suggestions, but you never fully let me know what was going on. When I finally talk you into getting help, you wind up getting drunk with your high school buddies, not to mention your old girlfriend. How could you find time for them and not me?"

Mike gulped as he processed this.

"Your text about the date made me feel like we were back on track, so I decided to surprise you. But when I got here and couldn't reach you, I bought a ticket from a scalper and tried to get backstage after the show. I was arguing with security when Jake saw me and got me in. He told me you'd gone back to the hotel with Jax, which I already wasn't happy about, and then I walk right into your crying ex-girlfriend. So, you tell me, Mike. What's going on?" she said, now weeping uncontrollably.

"June, honey. The truth is, I did tell her I'd always loved her, which gave her the wrong idea, and then she leaned in to kiss me. Obviously, I pulled away. Next thing I know she's taken off down the elevator, I was trying to catch her when I saw you guys together. Believe me when I say you and the kids are all I want," he said, pleading.

"Wait. What? You still love her?!"

"June," he said, grabbing her hand. "I love you. It was stupid to say that to her. For a moment, I wanted to be that teenager again. I'd just gotten done performing, and I got caught up in the nostalgia of it all. It was supposed to be a throwaway comment. I didn't mean it in a romantic way."

"I don't know, Mike. That's pretty big," she said and swiped her bangs away.

"June, please forgive me. You're right, I've been closed down and uncommunicative. Vance was coaching me, and we wound up at a restaurant for lunch. Then the old band walked in, and at first, I was trying to hide, but Vance convinced me to give them a chance and maybe heal our relationship."

"I wish you'd told me this earlier. Wait. What do you mean Vance was coaching you?"

"It's a long story, but it all has to do with the superconscious and understanding how to create the money and life we really want. He's been teaching me the secrets his grandfather taught him. He had me write down what I chose to create. One was performing with my band and another was to reconnect with you, which led to me performing tonight and why I texted you about the date. And as for tonight, you're right about that, too. I absolutely should have invited you. From your messages, I wasn't sure if you were still mad at me, but that's no excuse. I should have offered." He looked at his wife. "Come here," he said

As they hugged, June said, "Oh, Mike, it sounds like you've been having a wonderful couple of days, while I've been upset and worried."

"I know. I need to explain. Come upstairs, and let's talk."

On the ride up, Mike thought about how furious he was with Jax for lying and what an idiot he'd been for telling Jax how he loved her and nearly kissing her. This whole situation brought him back to reality and reminded him of who she really was. June could leave him over all of this. His unconscious wound was winning tonight, and he was inches from a wall.

He needed to reorient and focus on what he wanted. He visualized the happy marriage he desired and waited to get inspiration about exactly what to do next. By the time they'd reached the penthouse, he had his answer.

Once they got inside, he sat his wife down on the couch and explained the last two days he spent learning about structure and the superconscious process. How Vance had offered him the money, he'd declined it, and then Vance had given it to him anyway.

As June listened, she started to calm down.

"Wow, you've had quite an amazing couple of days," June said. "And we have fifty-thousand dollars?" she asked.

"We sure do," Mike replied with a smile.

"So, I was right then?" she asked, raising her eyebrows.

"You were right," Mike admitted.

"Ohhh, talk dirty to me. Say it again."

"You were right," Mike repeated. "Everything is going to turn out great."

"What a relief," June said. "And I never should have believed Jax's story. She was always two-faced and knew how to cause trouble. She was acting all dramatic, but I could tell she was lying. I was just so mad at you, I couldn't think straight."

Mike was so relieved. "Thank you," he said. "I'd forgotten how much she used to love to cause trouble. But I want you to understand that you're the only woman I love." Then he leaned over to give his wife a kiss.

"Ohhh, a kiss from a rock star," she teased.

Mike laughed. "Tonight's performance was something else, wasn't it?"

"I didn't know you had it in you," she said. "You were amazing. I remember seeing you perform a few times when we were kids, but nothing prepared me for tonight. You were so powerful, present and... really, really sexy," she admitted with a nervous laugh.

"Oh, was I?" Mike said with fake arrogance. "Tell me more about how sexy I am," he said, tickling her.

June was laughing hard. "You're the sexiest, middle-aged, punk-rocking psychologist I know!" she said cheekily.

They both laughed. It felt good to be reconnecting with his wife. Mike had forgotten just how much he loved spending time with her. Why had he shut her out?

"So, how does it feel to be married to this rock god?" Mike teased.

"Nearly as good as it feels to be married to a rich one!" June said with a smile. "Go on, show me the check!"

Mike got up and walked into the bedroom, feeling like everything was turning out perfectly. All of his choices were working out. This really was magic.

He grabbed his jeans and confidently went back to his wife.

"Here it is!" he declared.

Her reaction wasn't what he was expecting.

"Mike, you can't read this."

"What?"

"Look," she said, showing him the front of the check.

She was right. The writing was smudged. There was no way a bank would take this check. Mike's heart dropped.

"Ahh, no problem. I'll just ask Vance to write another one," he said.

"Of course!" June replied. "Let's get some sleep."

Mike agreed. It was well into the early hours of the morning, and he went to sleep with an uneasy feeling in his stomach. Would Vance write him another check? He sure hoped so.

He woke up the next morning at ten a.m. to the most beautiful sunrise and view over the whole city. Mike ordered room service and texted Vance about the check situation, which he rewrote a few times:

Vance, the concert last night was amazing. Thanks for everything. Unfortunately, the check got wet and smudged my name. Could I stop by to get another one?

Mike was angry at himself for getting the check wet, but it wasn't anyone's fault.

Vance texted back within minutes.

Where are you putting the power?

What do you mean? Mike texted back

Where you put your focus, energy flows. What structure are you in?

What? Mike couldn't believe it. Was Vance not going to write him another check?

His thoughts were interrupted by a knock at the door. "Room service!"

The guy wheeled in the full breakfast of coffee, orange juice, and the *Williamstown Daily News*. After he tipped the guy, he sat down and opened the paper, wanting to see if there was a review of the concert. He went straight to the Entertainment section and was pleased to see the headline: *Hometown Heroes Raging Crows Rocked The Revolver."*

There was a picture of all of them rocking out onstage. Next to that was one of Mike by himself, alongside another of his clinic. The one of him alone had the caption, *Punk-Rocking Psychologist, Dr. Michael Dunne*. He scanned the article, until he saw his name.

In an interview with lead singer Jake Rose, when asked if his bass player was really a doctor, Jake verified that he was Dr. Michael Dunne, a local psychologist, and shared about how he was an original member of the band when they started back in high school.

"We were so excited to have Dunny play with us again! We got lucky that he was able to fill in after our regular bassist broke his arm."

As Mike stared at the article in disbelief, June said, "Sally just sent me a link to a Raging Crows video. You look great!"

He walked over to look at June's phone. Because last night's performance was recorded by thousands of people, there was already a YouTube video of one of the band's most aggressive songs. Below it was a mixture of both positive and negative comments.

I read that the bass player's a psychologist. I'd never send my kid to a doctor like that.
A rockin' psychologist? Where do I sign up?
Will he still be able to keep his license?
I wonder what else he dresses up as?
With all that makeup, he has more problems than his patients.
Fuck yes! Rock and roll is my therapy!

June read along with him and said, "Who cares what a bunch of strangers think! You're still my rock god!"

Mike was concerned. He picked up his own phone and did a quick search for his name. Apparently, the story had made a lot of music websites, in addition to the paper. He then went to the online version of the article and saw the same kind of comments. It's amazing how people looking for something to be angry about will find it.

Mike slowly ate his breakfast as he processed it all. This wasn't good.

His phone rang, and he was pleased to see it was his nana.

"Michael, it's Nana. I see you're in the paper.! You look so happy!"

"Hi, Nana, yes, I had a great time," Mike replied.

"How are Jacob and Trevor? Did I see young Robert there as well? I haven't heard you speak of them in years. You never told me you were playing music again."

"They're great. It was a spontaneous thing, really. How are you?"

"Wonderful, dear. Gloria is so lovely. She says you're coming in for a meeting with her this week?"

That's right, Nan. I wish I had more time to talk. I promise I'll give you my undivided attention when I see you."

"Yes, yes. I understand. I can't wait. Love you. Bye."

Mike hung up and looked back at his wife.

"I wonder how this is going to affect business."

"I'm not sure, but all publicity is good publicity, right?" she asked with a smile.

"Guess we'll find out," Mike replied, before biting into his toast.

They enjoyed their breakfast while scrolling through different news outlets. Their breakfast was constantly interrupted by Mike's phone ringing with another friend or relative who'd seen the story.

"So, I was promised a date!" June said. "The kids are at my mother's all day."

Mike wasn't in the mood at all. He couldn't stop thinking about how bad everything was going to turn out., but he'd made a promise

"Go take a shower and get ready."

"Okay, but we'll have to go shopping first. The only clothes I have here are punk rock and definitely not day-at-the-beach material," she said, poking her tongue out and making a rocker sign with her fingers.

Mike put on a fake smile. The last thing he wanted to do was to spend more money or go on a date. He wanted to curl up and pretend all of this never happened. But then he remembered the thousand dollars he'd won at the track. It was going to feel great to spend that on his wife.

June danced off to the shower as Mike sat and took this all in. And now that he had time to think about it, he was also worried about Vance's response. What did "where is the power" mean?

Mike decided to open his notebook and reread his lessons from the first morning.

The unconscious wants to recreate conditions and circumstances it has survived before.

Mike laughed. Here he was, feeling powerless and needing to be saved. With what happened with Jax, the story in the paper, and the check being unusable, he was feeling rejected, powerless, and helpless to create what he wanted. It felt like he wasn't going to be able to save his grandmother. Everything was going wrong.

Could it be that he'd created this? Was it his unconscious working hard to create these circumstances?

He decided to take a step back from his experience and treat everything he was feeling and thinking as just one idea or opinion.

He started with Jax and the band. The truth was, he had an absolutely great night. He found out Jax never wanted to leave him, and just like when they were teenagers, she'd had found a way to stay in control by making up a story, which helped him shed his teenage rose-coloured glasses.

His initial response was that his relationship with the whole band was over. This was the same reaction he'd had many times, facing rejection, unable to please others. Running away from it seemed easier.

But that wasn't the truth, was it? He didn't want to run away.

He realized how his unconscious wound was sabotaging what he really wanted. He didn't know if Jax would repeat her story to his bandmates, but if she did, he'd deal with it. He wrote down his next action to plan a get-together with them.

His next challenge was how to deal with his newfound fame: Thinking about all the negative comments, he felt small and powerless, positive he'd never be able to make money as a psychologist again, which meant he'd never be able to support his family. He was angry at Jake for pulling him into the spotlight. And then he remembered his teachings.

Mike closed his eyes and experienced the fear of public humiliation. He felt the anger and worry build inside of him, letting himself get into a spin. Then he decided to put his focus on what he wanted to create and asked himself what his next action should be. He received an answer, which he said aloud to make it more concrete. "I would like to make great money and be a respected psychologist who changes lives."

Focusing his mind on this outcome, he asked for guidance from his intuition and received a genius idea. He could use the truth of the story to create good publicity. After all, this was about him stepping into his truth and letting go of the fear of what others think of him. Many of his current and would-be clients deny their own life desires and play it safe. Mike decided he would use this publicity to his advantage and contact the paper, offering to add to the story. He would spin it to be one about positivity and becoming who you were meant to be. The worst case would be that he would make a small amount of publicity worse, but maybe it would turn into something great.

He wrote down this action.

The next thing on his mind was Vance. His challenge was that the check was unusable, and Vance hadn't confirmed that he would replace it, so he might have to find a way to come up with the money.

What an idiot I am! He thought to himself. *It's so sad that I have to ask for another check. All I had to do was put it in my wallet. I'm just terrible with money.*

Following his internal tantrum, Mike thought about Vance's question regarding where he was putting the power, and the truth was, he was putting it in the wrong place. His biggest worry was how he would come up with the money for his grandmother. Without the check, he was screwed. He couldn't let his Nana down.

Mike had to figure something out, but how could he? With only a few days left, until he needed the money, there just wasn't enough time. Mike's stress levels were hitting the roof.

Surely Vance would replace the check, wouldn't he? But what if he didn't? What would Mike do then?

You need to snap out of this! You're staring at the wall.

Mike decided to ask himself the magic question. He said aloud, "What would I like to create?" The answer was obvious. To have enough money, so he could provide for his Nana.

He closed his eyes and visualized this result. After a minute or so, brought his attention back to the current situation to create the structure. Then, following the superconscious creation process, he asked for intuitive guidance as to what to do. Mike was surprised with the answer.

He received an image of his grandmother living at his house. She was happy and healthy. It didn't make sense. Mike closed his eyes and asked for guidance again regarding the money. After once again following the process, he received the same image. Maybe he was doing something wrong?

It didn't make sense. She couldn't live with them and be healthy. It meant no access to the care she needed.

He closed his eyes and visualized it again. He didn't want to admit it, but his superconscious guidance indicated that Nana needed to live with them. He was convinced this wasn't right, so he called Vance.

"Vance, it's Mike. I get what you mean now. I was putting the power in being saved again. I was feeling hopeless. I realized my mistake, so for the last ten minutes, I've been doing the superconscious creation process, and I've gotten amazing guidance on two of the three challenges I was facing. But with my Nana, I'm connecting to the end result of having enough money to ensure she's happy and healthy, and I keep getting a picture of her living with us, that just can't be right."

"Hi, Mike, good morning to you too." Vance chuckled. "I see you had a great night, you punk-rocking psychologist."

"So you saw the story?" Mike groaned.

"Sure did. I love the hair and makeup!" Vance joked. "So, back to your question. When it comes to superconscious guidance or intuition, you must learn to trust it. Your guidance seems to be the opposite to what your self-conscious believes needs to happen. But maybe having her live with you is the right answer. My advice is to trust your intuition."

Mike was still unsure. "It just sounds wrong."

Vance said, "Mike, I have to go. I'm actually on a plane right now to Italy. We're about to take off, and I'm getting looks to switch off my phone. Stay in your end result, and take the action your superconscious provides. It will all work out. Bye."

"Wait, Vance—" Mike said, but he'd already hung up.

Mike was scared to admit that having Nana at home would eliminate the huge financial stress, but he felt guilty. How could he let her down like this? She was supposed to be enjoying her golden years, and because of his inability to make money, she would suffer.

The truth was, he was stuck. The only option left was to use his house as collateral and get a second mortgage of sorts. But if he did that, it would activate his wife's deepest fears. It was like trading the health of his Nana for the health of himself and June. The added pressure of paying back a second mortgage, plus the stress of having a wife terrified of losing the home, would make life unbearable.

On the other hand, he could have his grandmother come live with them. She would be around family while he tackled the money problem and then getting her back into River Downs. Maybe it would only take a few months for him to figure everything out. That settled in his mind, Mike took a deep breath.

"It's obvious. Nana needs to move in with us," he said.

"What's that?" June asked, walking out of the bathroom, hair still wet and wrapped in a towel.

"Honey," Mike said, blinking back tears. "I've failed, and Nana needs to move in with us. I'm so sorry. I really tried, but this seems like my only option."

"Okay…" June said, sitting down and giving him a hug. "I've thought this is what would happen for a while now. I know you promised your grandfather you would look after her, but no one expected how much money everything would cost."

"Yes, I know. It's just that she's done so much for me, and I feel like I've let her down," Mike replied.

June grabbed Mike's hands and said in a stern voice, "Now you listen to me, Michael Dunne. All you do is look after everyone else. Providing for two children and coming up with a huge amount of money each year to look after your grandmother is no easy feat, especially in this economic climate. You have to look at the reality of the situation. In my opinion, running a psychology clinic that makes enough money to support your family and own a house that has enough room for your grandmother to move into, is very, very successful."

"Yeah, I guess," Mike admitted. "But I'm not giving up. I think having her with us will give me a little bit of space to figure out how to make the extra money. Maybe two or three months will be enough time. That's how long I'd planned to get the loan for anyway."

"This is why I love you. You're so committed to taking care of everyone. I appreciate you," June said with love. "I know you'll figure it out, and the kids are going to love having all the extra attention from their great-grandmother. She still has a lot of life left in her. I love you," June said, before standing up and giving him a kiss on the head. "It'll all be okay."

Mike looked back at the woman he loved who he'd been neglecting for far too long and almost lost due to his flawed memory of a teenage relationship. "I love you, June."

"I love you, too," June said and headed back into the bathroom, the noise of a hair dryer filling the air. Mike smiled. He loved that sound. It meant ten minutes of uninterrupted thinking. Mike smiled as he wrote down his next action.

Go see Nana, and tell her she'll be moving in with us.

Mike sat looking out the window of the penthouse suite. It was a beautiful view over the city. The mid-morning sun was nearly full in the sky, and for the first time in weeks, he felt relaxed. Each choice he'd written down that morning was going to be tough to accomplish, but the worst-case scenario of each one was manageable.

He glanced at his list and decided that he would action everything right now. The easy one was to text his bandmates. Surely they would be nursing hangovers right now, but they could reply to him whenever. He got his phone and sent a group text.

Guys, loved last night. How about we have a BBQ and jam session soon?

P.S. I'm happy to be your replacement bass player anytime.

Mike then grabbed the newspaper and noted the author of the article, Navi Khan. Phone still in hand, he went to the paper's website and found her email. He considered his words carefully before writing:

Subject: Punk-rocking psychologist

Hi, Navi

I'm Michael Dunne, the psychologist mentioned in your article about the Raging Crows.

After seeing comments made by the general public, I felt compelled to share my entire story.

If that's something you're interested in, please contact me through this email or my phone number below.

Regards,

Dr. Michael Dunne

PS: To sweeten the deal, I could also talk about how I broke the Vanderhill racetrack amateur lap time on Saturday.

Mike felt good to be in momentum and was pleased with how quickly he could pull himself out of a spin and get focused. He thought about how much he'd learned in just a few days, as he opened his book and examined his notes. Since he had time while June was drying her hair, he decided to sit and summarize what he'd learned.

- *Your life flows like water along the path of least resistance.*
- *Structure creates the path of least resistance.*
- *Your conscious focus creates your structure.*
- *There are three parts of your consciousness that all have a different agenda. The big conflict is between the self-conscious that wants to change, and the unconscious, that wants to stay the same.*
- *You can live in either the problem structure or the creative structure.*
- *The creative structure is focused on what you desire. The tension between your desire and current reality activates your superconscious superpower.*
- *The problem structure is focused on an unconscious wound. The tension between your wound and current reality activates unconscious strategies to try to avoid pain.*
- *In the problem structure, you never fully let go of the wound.*
- *Being all-in is necessary and takes courage.*
- *Becoming okay with the worst-case result and returning to innocence, allows you to refocus your structure.*
- *Everyone has a superpower. The superconscious creation process activates it.*
- *Going into a spin is inevitable. Focusing on what you want to create is the only way out of it.*
- *There are nine orientation points that create our reality. Each has a childhood wound, a strategy to avoid the wound, a superpower, and a basic desire.*

Mike sat back and looked at his notes, it really had been a whirlwind few days. He smiled, thinking about meeting Vance at the beach, Chow restaurant, the racetrack, the performance at The Revolver, and all the people he'd met. He could clearly see how each of the nine orientation points could either be stuck in the problem structure by taking action based on your wound, like Jax. Or flowing in the creative structure and creating magical results, like Suzi, Draymond, and Vance.

He now felt inspired to summarize each of the nine points, adding some extra thoughts from his previous research and experience. He thought about Nikola and his criticism about producing sub-standard beer. It was amazing how he turned this into his superpower to create No-Fear Beer.

First Orientation: The Perfectionist.
Superpower: perfection
Their wound is based on feeling bad or defective, evil, or corrupt, and their basic desire is to be good, virtuous, in balance, and have integrity. Their unconscious strategy is to create safety by being good, living to a high ideal and not making mistakes"

Mike thought that perfectly reflected Nikola's personality. And his brother Luka was a clear example of the third orientation. Super-driven to achieve and be the best. Mike chuckled to himself as he remembered the brothers' fiery argument.

Third Orientation: The Performer
Superpower: influence
Their wound is based on feeling worthless, without value apart from their achievements, and their basic desire is to feel worthwhile, accepted, and desirable. Their unconscious

strategy is to work hard to be successful and achieve what's impressive to others.

Mike thought about his amazing time onstage and the fiasco afterward. The fourth orientation had been on full display. The band had been in the superpower of this orientation, while Jax had been focused on her unconscious wound. He could see it was the same orientation, but culminating in a very different result. He could only hope Jax finds her way to her superpower.

Fourth Orientation: The Romantic
Superpower: emotion.
Their wound is based on feeling like they don't belong and have no identity or personal significance. Their basic desire is to find themselves and their significance, and create an identity out of their inner experience. Their unconscious strategy is to find themselves and live true to their uniqueness.

Mike recalled his conversation with Draymond and his abrupt departure.

Fifth Orientation: The Investigator
Superpower: focused intelligence.
Their wound is based on feeling helpless, useless, incapable, and overwhelmed, and their basic desire is to feel capable and confident. Their unconscious strategy is to learn everything they can and to understand it all thoroughly.

"I'm ready" June stated, interrupting Mikes train of thought.

Mike stopped what he was doing and looked over at his wife. "I just need ten minutes to finish this," he said

"What is it?"

"It's all the stuff I've learned from Vance about the super-conscious process" he said, holding up the book." I'm adding some extra clarity based on what I know as a psychologist. I can't wait to show you when I'm done."

"Okay, I'll call my mom and see how the kids are doing."

Mike smiled, realizing his wife was always making sure her loved ones were safe. She was a clear example of the sixth orientation. He loved how loyal she was. She was perfect for someone like him, who was always worried about people leaving them.

Man, I'm lucky, he thought to himself, before getting back to the task at hand.

Sixth Orientation: The Loyalist
Superpower: safety
Their wound is based on feeling they have no support and guidance and are unable to survive on their own. Their basic desire is to find security and support, and their unconscious strategy is to know who and what to believe in and that they will be okay if they do what's expected.

Mike thumbed through his book to find the description of the seventh orientation, Suzi, the enthusiastic creator.

Seventh Orientation: The Enthusiast
Superpower: invention
Their wound is based on a belief that it's bad to be sad or negative. Their basic desire is to be happy, satisfied, and ful-filled. Their unconscious strategy is to always be happy, have

lots of ideas and interests, and to never stay in one place or relationship too long for it to feel boring.

And of course, how could he forget Vance's orientation?

Eighth Orientation: The Protector
Superpower: power.
Their wound is based on a feeling harmed, controlled, or violated by others, and their basic desire is to protect themselves and determine their own course in life. Their unconscious strategy is to be strong and in control of everything.

This must be why he loves being the CEO of a worldwide organization.

Then Mike took a deep breath, knowing he was about to face the music. He wrote out his own orientation.

Second Orientation: The Helper
Superpower: knowing what others need
Their wound is based on feeling unloved and unwanted, and ending up alone, and their basic desire is to feel loved. Their unconscious strategy is to make everyone else happy.

Mike understood that he definitely lived this unconscious wound and wondered how he'd use his superpower to create what he wanted.

"It's been ten minutes. Let's go!" June said impatiently.

"Just one more minute, promise."

Ninth Orientation: The Peacemaker
Superpower: harmony.

Their wound is based on feeling overlooked, and that conflict and chaos are painful. Their basic desire is to create peace and maintain peace of mind. Their unconscious strategy is to have no defined goals and to ensure everyone gets along.

"Okay, I'm done! Let's go!"

He and June had a fantastic, relaxing Sunday together. They went shopping, walked on the beach, and ate ice cream. In the afternoon, they picked up the kids and had a connected family dinner, where everyone laughed at Mike's punk rock moment and scrolled pictures on June's phone.

Even though nothing had changed in his current reality, Mike felt focused and excited about the week ahead. He had business meetings set up with some of the most successful people in town, a journalist hopefully banging down his door for an interview, and he was going to remove the stress of his River Downs financial burden. He finally felt like things were working out for him. The best part was, no one was saving him but himself, though he did still wonder how he would use his superpower to create magic.

CHAPTER TWELVE

THE MAGIC OF THE SUPERCONSCIOUS CREATION PROCESS

Mike woke up excited. He got to work early and was surprised by the volume of emails. Not only did Navi want an interview, but so did a couple of other news outlets. There were also new inquiries and a few disgruntled clients wishing to cancel or refund their appointments. Mike was expecting it all. He was ready.

He replied to the news outlets right away, handled the unhappy clients, and booked in the inquiries for their first appointment.

On the button at nine a.m., the noise started, with the buzz of a tattoo gun and the occasional scream of pain echoing through the wall.

Mike clenched his fists.

Then a few minutes later, the adult shop's animated show started.

"Why would anyone go to a place like that?" he grumbled to himself.

But he didn't have long to get annoyed, as his phone started ringing and didn't stop for the next hour. By the time he sat down with his first patient of the day, Mike had scheduled an interview with motivated Navi.

The day flew by, and before he knew it, he was sitting down in his office with Navi Khan from the *Williamstown Daily News*. According to her bio, Navi was a twenty-something-year-old motivated journalist who was also a swimsuit model and online influencer. She wrote about popular culture, music, and local events. Navi was a true socialite in every sense of the word, totally connected.

"Dr. Dunne, great to meet you," Navi said, starting off the conversation professionally.

"Yes, you too. Would you like tea or coffee?" Mike asked.

"No, I'm good, thank you. I have my kombucha here," she said, pointing to some weird-shaped bottle. Mike knew of the stuff. June even got him to try it one time. He wasn't a fan.

"Plus, I won't be staying long," Navi added. "But I'd love to ask you a few questions for a follow-up article."

"Shoot," Mike replied.

"It looks like your gig on Saturday was a success. We only popped in to get a few pictures, and the energy in that venue was unbelievable. The crowd was wild," she said.

"Yes, very intense," Mike replied with a smile.

Navi unpacked the contents of her bag onto the table while making small talk.

"You also mentioned that you race cars and broke some sort of record? That's impressive. Wasn't it raining on Saturday?" she asked.

"It certainly was! It was quite dangerous, actually." Mike shook his head and laughed.

"Would you mind if I live streamed this interview? I have nearly a million followers who would love to take part in this."

"Absolutely," Mike replied.

Navi whipped out her phone, and in less than a minute, the small streaming studio was set up. She'd clearly done this a few times.

"You ready?" she asked.

He nodded. "Let's do this."

Navi pressed "go live," and they were off.

"Welcome, everybody. Today we have a special guest. I'm here with Dr. Michael Dunne, the punk-rocking psychologist who was featured yesterday in our article about the Raging Crows." As Navi turned to Mike, he noticed her energy changed significantly. "So, Dr. Dunne, it looks like you had one heck of a Saturday night, performing live with the Raging Crows."

"Sure did. It was a night I'll never forget," he replied.

"Yeah, I bet. It seems quite different from what you do every day. Was this a normal Saturday for you?" Navi asked.

"No, not at all. In fact, like Jake said in the article, the normal bass player got injured," he said with a smile.

"Right. Jake said you were one of the founding members. It's probably how you were able to fill in on such short notice."

"Well, I'm a big fan as well, and I keep up with them. But yeah, we started the band in high school, and I was a member, until I took off for college. It was a long time ago, probably before you were born," Mike joked.

"Ah, I see. You love this kind of music!" Navi's smile was predatory, and Mike guessed he wasn't going to like what she said next. "So, Dr. Dunne, the big question on everyone's mind is, what makes it okay for a clinical psychologist to enjoy a band that promotes anger and violence?" she asked in an accusing tone, and Mike couldn't gather his thoughts in time, before she said, "How can you guide troubled people, knowing you like to promote anger and violence?"

Mike took a sip of water. He could feel his blood boiling. She'd obviously come prepared to do a hit piece, and he knew he had to refocus before he ended up in a spin. He was, after all, streaming live to over a million people, so he quickly refocused on what he wanted to create from the interview.

"Thank you for your insightful question that I'm sure many people want to hear the answer to," he said. "So, you want to know what makes it okay for a psychologist to enjoy and perform that music?"

"Yes," she replied.

"Great, because I think it's vital to understand that most people deny their true nature. They're so focused on who and what they should be in order to gain the approval of others, they've become lost and unable to figure out what they truly want. In our society, we see ourselves and our life as a problem that needs to be solved. We're driven by something called our unconscious wound, to try and gain what we think we're missing. This fear leads many to addictively try to fix, heal, or do enough to finally be allowed to experience what they want in life. When I talk to my patients—"

"Okay, thanks for that," Navi said, cutting him off. "But you didn't answer the question. We saw you onstage drinking straight from a vodka bottle, promoting aggression and violence. How can we trust you with our most vulnerable and in-need people?"

"Let me address your first point. If you'd taken the time to look up our lyrics, you'd discover that most of them are actually about standing up for yourself and not taking crap from people. But yes, some of them are violent. They were written when we were all focused on our unconscious wound and didn't know any better."

"I'm sorry, what does that mean?"

"Let me give you an example. I lost my parents when I was seven, which created an unconscious wound of being abandoned by the people I love and the need to save. Now, while it wasn't my fault that I lost my parents, my unconscious kept replaying this experience into adulthood. In my practice, I see this all the time. We all use strategies to avoid this unconscious wound, creating beliefs and rules about how we should be and what we need to do to avoid pain. And because we know how to survive these painful, wounding experiences, we keep recreating them. People are focused on drama and problems, unconsciously believing they can't live the life they love. For instance, you're stuck in an unconscious wound."

"Me?" Navi said indignantly. "I'm doing just fine, thank you."

"Yes. It's why instead of focusing on all the positive songs, or the fact that I stepped in on late notice and crushed the performance, you decided to concentrate on the negative angle."

"I still don't know what you're talking about."

"I'll get to that in a minute. Let me address your question about how people can trust someone like me." Mike took another drink of water, fully tuning into his superconscious power. "I run two businesses, have a stable and happy marriage, and I'm a father of two great kids. I'm also someone who's not scared of being who they are. Who doesn't just talk the talk but also walks the walk. Who in one day broke a racetrack record and went on to perform in front of a sold-out crowd. Are you saying that people should only trust a doctor who does nothing but sit in their office pretending they're perfect? I'm imperfect and happy to admit it. I feel anxious at times. For instance, right now I'm worried I won't have enough money to pay for my grandmother's medical bills." Mike paused and stared Navi down. "Now, how about you answer your own question. Do you think people can trust someone like that?"

Navi cleared her throat. "What about the drinking?"

Mike laughed. "Yeah, I might have had a few drinks, but I'm a family man with responsibilities, it's not the way I usually spend my evenings. But to get back to my point, playing music in front of a sold-out audience has been my lifelong dream. I was asked to perform mere hours before I took the stage, and I was terrified, but I followed through, overcame my fear, and performed at my best. If you were asked to fulfill your lifelong dream and only had two hours to prepare, would you do it?"

Navi was looking more and more uncertain. Clearly, the interview had gotten away from her. This was someone who was used to nailing people to the wall and loved doing it.

"I don't know," she said.

"Navi, my clients come to me with all sorts of issues, but the underlying cause of everything is that they're not going for what they love. They see themselves as broken, needing fixing, healing, and improvement, but the best therapy is for them to focus on creating a life they love." He smiled. "So, Navi, if you had all the money in the world, and if you knew you couldn't fail, what would be the one thing you'd want to create or experience more than anything else?"

She took a deep breath and replied, "I would start a charity for the survivors of domestic violence."

"Great, that's an amazing thing to do," Mike replied. "It's really needed, especially today, with things like cyberbullying, where your abuser doesn't even need to be in the same room to traumatize you."

"That's true."

"Okay, so since you haven't done that, I can only assume there are people who are hurting because of your inaction, right? There has to be. If it's needed, and you're not doing it, then your inaction is causing pain."

"I guess you're right," Navi said, seeming to process this information.

"So, what's stopping you?" Mike asked. "It's clearly not about having enough money, because even if all your followers just donated something small, like two dollars, you would have millions. So, it must be that you're too scared to fail. I see it all the time. Instead of going for what you love, you're distracted by pointing out what everyone else is doing wrong. It's exactly what brought you in here today."

"No. I was really offended by your lyrics. I'm sensitive to abuse, and your lyrics are abusive."

"Navi, I get it, but you went on the attack right away. It's obvious you didn't do any research, or you might have picked out specific songs and asked me what they meant."

Navi bowed her head. "You might have a point."

"I don't blame you for your criticisms. It's not your fault. So many people concentrate on the problem, but the only truly happy and successful people are those who let go of that reality. So, to answer your question, other than being a fully qualified doctor with years of experience, people should trust me, because I'm willing to dig for the truth. I would never tell a patient to do anything I wouldn't, or haven't, done. I'm not the enemy. I've been where you are, with a big dream but feeling too scared to push myself, worried about what people thought of me and pretending through my life. But I've learned some things about myself in the last few days, like how to follow my intuition. If I can do one thing with this fifteen minutes of fame I've been given, it's to let people know that rather than trying to figure out how they're broken, they should devote their energy to creating a life they love. If you focus on what you would really like to create and hold your focus you can turn your wounds into your superpower."

"Superpower?" Navi asked.

"Yes, we all have one. Yours is clearly the superpower of influence. But like I said, each superpower is borne out of a wound. If I'm right, yours would be feeling like you're not enough, unless you achieve something. You're probably addicted to achieving without it ever being satisfying. But with a bit of education and training, you can learn to get in the right frame of mind to activate your superpower."

"Is that what you teach in your sessions?" Navi asked.

I will from now on." Mike paused then said, "Navi, if you or any of your listeners would like to know more, I'm going to be putting together a seminar on this exact topic. Can I tell you a little about it" Mike asked, letting his superpower of knowing what others need take over.

"Yes, I would love that," Navi replied, leaning in.

"At the seminar you'll learn how to unleash your potential. You will learn to truly know yourself, so you can step into your full power. This is one of the greatest gifts, because you'll know exactly when you're giving the power to your unconscious wound, which will allow you to switch into a different structure."

"Structure?"

I'll teach more about this at the seminar, but a structure is anything that has two or more parts held together by tension. Whenever there's a discrepancy in the tension, there's movement to bring it back to equilibrium. So, we can live in the creative structure, which is your current reality and what you want to create, or the problem structure, which has to do with your current reality and an unconscious wound.

"That sounds interesting. I'd love to learn more about that."

"Great. I'll also talk about not falling victim to your unconscious wound, and how by trying to fix or heal it, you give the power to what you don't want. Many people have spent a lifetime trying to heal themselves and never realize that if they just put that same focus on the end result, their issues will no longer be a problem. The key is to observe the unconscious agenda, notice how it's trying to solve a fear from childhood, and then let it go."

Navi nodded. "This is a lot to take in, but I think I understand."

"All successful people have figured out how to stay focused on the outcome instead of trying to fix or change themselves, which allows their genius to emerge. Because of this connection, they create art, music, poetry, technology, new education, inventions, and everything beautiful we have in our world. Remember, every invention was once an idea in the mind of the person or people who created it. We're all creators, but due to our unconscious wounds, we've forgotten this part of ourselves, because we're caught up in trying to solve where we feel hurt. Does that make sense?"

"I think so. You're basically saying that most other psychologists have people focused on the problem, but this does nothing but make it more powerful. If people learned to focus on what they really want and are brave enough to take action, we would have more happy people...and more punk-rocking psychologists?" she said with a smile.

Mike laughed. "For sure. What I'm describing is the super-conscious creation process. I used it to win at the racetrack and also perform live in front of an audience for the first time in twenty years. Did you know I'd never played most of those songs with the band before?" Mike asked.

"No, I didn't. You looked so natural up there," Navi replied.

"I'd put off playing music live and reconnecting with my old friends for years, because I was stuck in my unconscious wound. Since my parents died, my unconscious has been try-ing to make sure I never lose anyone again. These beliefs led me to a life of denying my own desires and focusing on making sure everyone else was taken care of. It doesn't work. I see the unconscious wound and strategy in all of my patients. The truth is, the more power they put in trying to fix or avoid what they're scared of, the more they get stuck. It's a total epidemic in our culture. It's everywhere."

Navi nodded. "This is true, especially now. Because of so-cial media, everyone is constantly comparing themselves to others, thinking they're not worthy"

"I was one of those people. I was frustrated and stuck, re-senting those who'd achieved success. But now I know what it's like to reorient my life and create spectacular results. It would be great if you wrote about how in this society, we have everything, and yet we find it impossible to be happy. Like you said, people compare themselves to others. This is because we feel we're lacking some essential ingredient the other person has, when in reality, we're perfectly capable of achieving the same level of success."

"That makes sense," Navi replied. "

Mike looked directly at the camera and confidently said, "How many of you would love to finally create the life of your dreams and are courageous enough to let go of the way you have been??"

Hundreds of replies came in an instant.

Mike's heart swelled. "I'm so happy you're all on board. Navi will enter my email into the chat. Please contact me to get on the waiting list for my first workshop."

Mike handed Navi a card, and she typed out the address. "Thank you so much, Dr. Dunne."

"My pleasure. I want you all to know that I'm just like you. I'm a humble teacher. I'm imperfect. I've spent a lifetime focused on my unconscious wound and over twenty years being the perfect doctor who helped everyone else. But the truth is, I do love playing the bass, and I love punk rock. I also have a passion for helping people. I desire both. But just like you and everyone watching, when faced with an opportunity to fulfill my biggest dream, I nearly didn't take it. You see, about two hours before the show, I had a huge argument with myself. One part of me wanted to run home. I was worried about the exact judgment you came in here with today," he said.

"I can understand that" Navi said.

"I thought I would lose my family and my clinic." He laughed "It's ridiculous how much our unconscious wound controls us. I was so caught up in these beliefs, my unconscious made up this whole story. The funny thing is, I'm close to losing it all anyway."

"How so?" Navi asked.

"Well, because of that noise," he said, pointing to the walls. The sound of the adult shop and tattoo parlour was as loud as ever. "I can't work here like I used to."

"I was wondering about that," Navi said.

"Do you see what I mean? The unconscious tried to stop me from following my heart to lose something that was nearly lost anyway."

"Wow... you really do know yourself. I wish I had that clarity." Navi said.

"It's possible. I'm hoping to see you at my seminar."

"How are we all doing out there?" she asked, turning toward the livestream.

The comments flowed faster than Mike could read them, and then he looked at his watch.

"Navi, I'm sorry, I have to end our session." He smiled. "I need to get across town to see my grandmother. Let's continue this another time?" he asked, standing.

"Yes, sounds great." Navi turned to her livestream. "Well, that was an unexpected and interesting conversation. Tune in next time for more of what's happening in your town. That was punk-rocking psychologist Michael Dunne, and this is Navi Khan, signing off."

Mike walked Navi out. He had to say goodbye fast. River Downs didn't let people visit after six p.m. He had a very small window of time to get to the other side of town.

As he zoomed through traffic, Mike's mind raced just as fast.

Where did all of that come from? He'd been so confident and articulate. Usually, he struggled with any sort of presentation or public speaking, and needed hours of practice and cue cards. But he'd just conducted a livestream interview to a million people. It could have gone so wrong. He laughed, thinking about what Navi's intention must have been at the start. And what was all that about a workshop? He'd only just been given this information. How could he teach it?

But it all felt right. Is that what Vance meant about innocence? The thought of running a workshop was exciting. It was like combining his love of performing music and teaching people. It was actually genius.

Mike's internal celebration didn't last long. He was nearly at the retirement home and had no idea how he was going to tell his grandmother the unfortunate news.

But he knew what to do. For the rest of the drive, he was only going to focus on one thing: a happy and healthy family. That's what he chose to create and was the only thing that mattered. He wondered what magic the superconscious would come up with.

By the time he got to River Downs, he walked in with confidence, signed in at reception, and made his way to his grandmother's room.

After knocking, he said softly, "Nana, are you there?"

"Michael, is that you?"

He walked in to find her in her large La-Z-Boy recliner. She switched off the TV and turned to face him. She had a knitted blanket around her and looked so peaceful and happy. The moment was too much for him, and he started to choke up.

"Hi, Nana, yes, it's me," he said with a smile. "Your favourite grandson." He walked over to give her a hug and a kiss. "How are you?"

"I'm good," she replied enthusiastically. "How are June and the kids?"

"So great. June and I had an amazing time at the beach yesterday."

"And how is my punk-rocking grandson?" she asked with a smile.

"Ha, I'm great, Nan, really great. I've had one heck of a week. It's unbelievable, really. It all started last time I visited you and had coffee with Gloria. A gentleman named Giovani Vanderhill overheard my conversation, and it turned out his cousin is Vance Vanderhill."

"Oh, Giovani, how is he?" Nana asked. "I saw him the other day. He waved through the window while you were in here with me. He must have been visiting someone. I was hoping to catch him before he left, but we missed each other. Did you know he was a friend of your grandfather's when they were younger?"

Mike nodded. "He mentioned that."

"We used to have a lot to do with the Vanderhills. It's nice to hear their names."

"Well, Giovanni suggested I meet his cousin and said he could help me." Mike laughed. "I was doubtful, but I called anyway."

"Oh? And was he able to help you?

"Actually, I learned a lot from him," Mike replied.

"That's great to hear. I'm glad he turned out well."

"Me, too. So, you know Vance?"

"Yes, when Vance was a child, well before you were born. Your grandfather used to do work around the Vanderhill house, and he became good friends with the whole family. Vance's father wasn't a very nice man. He had a real problem with drugs and alcohol. I'm not sure what happened, but all I know is that your pop came home one day from playing cards, and he was so angry. He told me all about Vance's father and the abuse he witnessed. Apparently, your pop stepped into an argument between Vance's parents. He left his phone number and told the kids to call him if anything like that happened again. Your pop was a good man. He always did what was right and stood up for those who couldn't," she said, beaming with pride. "The kids called a few times over the years, and your grandfather would go over there. I think it really helped your grandfather grieve the loss of your father. It was so hard for him to lose his son, but he ended up taking an interest in Vance's life."

"Really? I don't remember him at the funeral," Mike said.

"Well, he and your grandfather had a big argument about fifteen years ago. It had to do with some information that Vance wanted to teach him. Apparently, he'd figured out the secrets of the Universe or something, but your grandfather didn't want to hear it. Your pop, as you know, was a devout religious man who was head of the workers' union and very stubborn. He was totally against any ideas that seemed to challenge his way of thinking."

"He sure was stubborn," Mike replied with a smile.

"Yes, he was," Nana said, laughing. "I think at one stage, Vance offered to invest in any business Pop wanted to start. Said he'd give him an interest-free loan. This was apparently so offensive to your grandfather that he broke off any communication with him. I guess Vance didn't feel welcome at the funeral. Anyway, you were telling me about your week?"

"Right. So, when I met up with him, he offered to help me with a challenge I'm facing. The last few days have been a blur, to be honest. I drove in a Lotus on the racetrack, where I found out I beat the amateur record. Then I rocked out in front of a sold-out crowd with my old band and wound up a featured story in the local news. It was a week to remember," Mike said, grinning ear to ear. "Hey, would you like some tea?" Mike asked.

"Yes, dear, that would be great," Nana replied.

Mike needed a moment to think. He made his way over to the small kitchen, filled the electric kettle, and turned it on

It all made sense now. This is why Vance wanted so badly to help. If Pop had taken the investment, would Nana be in this situation? Knowing he had multiple chances to turn his life around, Mike realized that his grandparents didn't accidentally fall into their financial situation, they created it.

Before this moment, Mike had bought into the stories his grandfather told him about his blue-collar roots and that the working class could never get ahead, because of the evil capitalists. He now knew his grandparents probably had many chances to step into a different structure, but didn't.

He finished making the tea and walked back over to sit down with his grandmother.

"Nana, if you could live the rest of your life in any way, what would you choose?"

"Easy. I would like to be healthy and young again. Oh, and for your grandfather to be alive. I've been lost without him. And your parents. I would want them back. No parent should ever have to witness their child die. It's just not right!" she replied.

"Yes, true, we all would like that," he said, realizing he needed to rephrase the question. "But since that's impossible, how would you like to live the rest of your life? What would you like to create?".

"That's a strange question, Michael." She thought for a moment before responding, "I don't know. If I didn't have this stupid disease, I would like to spend as much time with you, June, and my great-grandchildren as possible."

"You would?" Mike said, surprised. "Wouldn't you want to travel? See the world? Go on cruises? Learn something new?" he asked.

"Oh, no," Nana said, laughing. "Not at all. I've seen the world. Traveling at my age wouldn't be as much fun. What I miss the most is having family around. You know? The little things, like making dinner, playing cards, watching TV together, doing the dishes, and hearing what everyone did during their day. That's what I want the most."

Mike took a deep breath. "Nana, I need to confess something. The cost of River Downs and your treatment is putting too much financial stress on me, and I've failed to come up with the money. I feel terrible about it. Like I've let you and Pop down. But it's the unfortunate truth." Mike hesitated then said, "June and I have been talking, and we think you moving in with us is the best option to give me some breathing space to get the finances together. And in the meantime, you'll get your wish about spending more time with us," he said.

"Oh, Michael, I'm grateful to have a grandson like you," Nana said in a comforting tone, before reaching over and squeezing his hand. "You make me so proud. And I know your pop and your parents would be delighted with the man you've become. None of us could have predicted this disease and the treatment I'd need. The truth is, your grandfather and I didn't save enough to cover this. It's not your fault. The last thing I want in the world is to be causing you extra stress. Come here and give me a hug," she said.

Mike could feel the release of pressure in his chest as he leaned in to give his nana a hug.

"Michael, I would happily move in with you. That's more than enough for me. I don't want to hear anything else about it. I'm actually excited about this!" Nana beamed.

Mike appreciated his grandmother's enthusiasm, and he knew that she wanted to spend more time with the family, but could they give her the proper around-the-clock care she needed? Here there were nurses on staff should anything go wrong, which comforted him. Only time would tell. So even though this could be a good thing, he still felt like he'd failed.

Also, Vance had said he'd take care of Nana's medication, and he felt confident the billionaire wouldn't back out on his promise.

"Thanks, Nana. Yes, it's going to be fun," he muttered against his true feelings.

Mike pushed all of his misgivings aside to give Nana his full attention. They sat together and enjoyed their tea, talking about what room she would move into, the kids' schedule of sporting activities, and what time they went to school. Nana was hoping she'd be well enough to help out June. She said she wanted to contribute to the household. His nana seemed honestly excited about the whole idea.

Afterward, Mike headed home. He'd made a promise to himself that he would figure out the money situation, but to do it in a way that he didn't lose his family. He knew he could have it all. He felt positive everything would work out.

Mike walked out to the car and decided to send Vance the text.

Vance, I don't need the check. I'll take the education and put the power in my own end result.

Vance replied instantly.

Best decision you will ever make. It will be worth much more than $50K. Well done.

But I did promise to take care of your nana, so if I need to help with her medication, please let me know.

Mike drove home filled with internal turmoil. Part of him wanted to just call Vance back and get the check, but he was committed to living in a new structure. He felt good that Vance reiterated his promise. This wasn't the same as him taking a huge check for himself. Besides, if Vance offered without hesitation, he knew he was on the right path.

Now that he'd gotten one situation taken care of, his mind wandered to other loose ends. He never heard back from the band. It was such a pleasure playing in front of that crowd, but what a terrible way to end an amazing night. He had so many unanswered questions. Did Jax say something to them? Did she continue with the same lie she told June? Will it ruin his chances of playing with the band again?

Mike noticed he was going into a spin, so he decided to refocus on what he wanted: to play with the band again and to rekindle their long-lost friendship

He had Jake's number and was stuck in traffic. There was no reason not to call. He took a big breath and hit the button. After a couple of rings Jake answered.

"Dunny, how are you, bro?"

"I'm great, but my correct title is now punk rocking psychologist" Mike replied tongue in cheek.

"Oh, yeah. I guess I let the cat out of the bag," Jake replied. "Couldn't have predicted she'd take what I said and run with it."

"I had the time of my life! I'd love to do it all again" Mike said, conscious that Jake didn't seem annoyed with him at all.

"Yes, absolutely. We have some gigs scheduled for later in the year, but let's catch up before then. How about a barbecue? Love to meet your family!" Jake said with enthusiasm

"Sounds great," Mike replied.

Hey, is Jax there? I'd like to talk to her," Mike said.

Yeah, sure. Speak soon. Jake said.

"Hey, Mike," Jax said in a defeated tone, like she'd been summoned to the principal's office

Mike worked up a level of enthusiasm he didn't feel and said, "Hey, Jax! Just wanted to catch up with you. Saturday was amazing, wasn't it? Shame the drinks got the best of us at the end there. Sorry for that. I think everyone was so excited to see each other after all these years," Mike said.

"Yea, I had a lot to drink," Jax replied. "Sorry about that. Is June okay?"

"She is! No harm done. Look, let's leave it all behind us? Jake and I were just talking about getting together for a barbecue. What do you think?"

"Sounds great!" Jax replied in a relieved tone.

"Cool. I'll talk to June and organize a time with Jake. Can you let the others know?"

"Sure can!"

"Great, see you soon!"

It took every ounce of his focus to not accuse Jax of trying to ruin his marriage and demand an apology. That wouldn't have led to his desired end result. He was proud of his new ability to stay focused on what he truly desired and take the correct action. He was becoming really good at getting out of a spin.

He also considered telling Jake what happened himself but figured it would do more harm than good.

Mike drove the rest of the way home making an internal commitment to always focus on the end result, rather than buckling to the tension of his unconscious to blame and judge or run away.

"How did it go?" June asked as Mike walked in the front door.

"Good, actually. Nana really loves the idea. I was surprised."

"That's great, honey," June said wrapping her arms around him and giving him a big hug. "I'm so proud of you"

"Thanks, I'm not really proud of the result, to be completely honest, but I know Nana will be thrilled to spend time with us."

Nana moved in later that week, and the impact on the household was positive. Nana was full of energy, it seemed. The frail, forgetful woman seemed to disappear, and after a month of her steadily regaining her strength, the family was thriving.

She allowed Mike and June to get so much more out of life. She'd watch the kids, which allowed them a date night out by themselves. Nana decided that two nights a week she would cook, and was making school lunches for the kids most days. Mike would often come home to Nana singing as she cleaned the kitchen or hung out some washing. Most days, she would walk down to the shop and buy fresh groceries.

Mike watched his nana closely to see if she'd fall back into the brain fog she'd been experiencing, and he'd have to call Vance, but so far, it seemed her current medication was working. In fact, her brain was so sharp now, she would help the kids with homework. She taught the children how to play cards instead of watching TV each night, and there was a competitive battle between the three of them. The family had never been happier.

June had more time available and increased her hours at work, which allowed them to pay for little luxuries and expenses like braces for Bec. Because of the extra time, June was also able to restart her salsa dancing classes, and the added exercise caused her to lose some weight, so she was feeling great.

Mike had the space to focus on his work. Every day he would follow the superconscious creation process. He'd give up needing to know the answer, close his eyes, and visualize the end result. Then he would ask for guided, inspired action, and take it. He wouldn't let his unconscious wound steal his focus, no matter what. Because of his new outlook, some magical changes started taking place.

He approached his neighbouring businesses to figure out a solution for the noise. Because of his direct conversation, the animated peep show was moved to the other side of the building. He then worked with a local sound engineer and the tattoo parlour to use cheap egg trays spray-painted black to soundproof the other wall. On top of reducing the noise, he also played baroque music in the background of his clinic. This was enough to ensure his patients were happy.

Mike's workshop offer on Navi's show garnered a lot of attention, and he was sold out in no time. As the event got closer, he began to worry. He knew the content was exactly what people needed, but there was one problem. This was Vance's information. He hadn't heard from the billionaire in weeks, and this made him uncomfortable, but he decided to proceed anyway.

After multiple texts, emails, and phone calls, Vance finally replied a day before his first workshop.

Mike, sorry I've taken so long to get back to you. You're more than welcome to share the information. This is our work. It's for everyone. I'm in the end result of people learning this information. I would love for you to share it in any way you think is correct. You have my full blessings.

Mike received the message a few hours after it was sent. He phoned Vance, hoping to thank his mentor and share in the success he was having. No one really knew what Mike went through to let go of the problem structure and trust his super-conscious superpower like Vance did. But it wasn't to be. Vance didn't pick up.

After weeks of waiting, it was finally time for his workshop. Mike was nervous but excited. He woke up early and had breakfast with his family, before they all piled into the car. It was a full family affair, with everyone pitching in to help. June registered guests as they arrived, and the kids ushered people to their seats, while Nana looked after the tea and coffee station.

Over a hundred people were packed into the conference room, and right at ten a.m., Navi gave the introduction for Mike to take the stage. The topic of the workshop was "The Superconscious Creator Code: How to Find Your Power and Create a Life You love." He poured his heart into teaching everything he knew, and when the day was done, there was a huge mass of people lined up to thank him and tell him how excited they were to go and implement it.

Mike had no words for the joy he felt in his heart to share this information. He knew this was his calling and decided to do everything he could to share it with the world.

He seemed to have a never-ending stream of people wanting to learn from him, the punk-rocking, race-car-winning psychologist. He was starting to really build a following. Each workshop, the people who attended the event would get so inspired, they'd tell their friends. This led to more people buying tickets, and he had requests to do the workshop across the country, and even write a book.

He was in big momentum. The only problem he was worried about was his nana. Though she seemed to be thriving, he was always waiting to see if she'd relapse, and she wouldn't be able to get the proper care she needed. He decided that when he did get the money together, his grandmother would split her time living with them and River Downs. It had been so positive having her around, it made no sense to stop it. Splitting her time meant she could get the care she needed and also enjoy family time. It would be perfect.

After four months, Mike completed his tenth sold-out workshop. He'd saved every penny, and because each workshop was netting a profit of a few thousand dollars, he had more than enough to pay for River Downs, and he knew he could afford it in the future.

He sent Vance a text message:

Vance!!! I did it. I have the money for Nana. It's MAGIC!

Mike raced home. He'd been waiting for this day for months and was overwhelmed with pride in himself. This was incredible. He had everything he'd written down on that first day with Vance. It was too much for him to handle, and the tears streamed down his face. He turned on the radio to the song "We are the Champions," by Queen, and he belted it out as loud as he could through tears as he drove home triumphant.

Walking in the door, he was greeted by an excited June, who wore a huge smile. Then she looked at his tear-stained face and said, "Have you already heard?"

"Heard what?"

"That Nana is free of the disease!" Bec yelled from behind her.

"Wait. What?" Mike asked, walking inside.

Seated at their dining room table was his grandmother, grinning from ear to ear, holding a medical report. She handed the papers to Mike, who read that she was in remission, and there were no signs of any symptoms for over two months.

"What? You don't have it anymore?" he asked, sitting down. "I can't believe this."

"It's true, Michael. I've been keeping it quiet, so no one got their hopes up. But after three months of negative results, the doctors have assured me it's true. It's a miracle."

"But how can this be?" Mike said in shock. ".

Mike's phone rang. It was Vance.

"Vance! You're not going to believe this!" Mike said.

"Mike, I just got your text. Well done. That is some magical creation!" Vance said with excitement. "Wahooo! It's so great to see you living the superconscious path!"

"You haven't even heard the full story. I just got home to tell my family, and they informed me that we have more reason to celebrate. My grandmother has spontaneously recovered and has been symptom-free for two months! It looks like she won't need the meds after all!" Mike said.

"Now that's some magic," Vance replied. "The unconscious is strong, isn't it?"

"What do you mean?" Mike asked.

"Well, didn't your Nana come down with the disease right after your grandfather died?" Vance asked.

"Yes, she did."

"If I remember your grandmother, she was always focused on looking after others. With no one to take care of, I guess her unconscious created a disease, so she needed to look after something. Once she moved in with you, I'm sure she had more to do in life, and the unconscious strategy wasn't needed anymore! Who knows, but wow!" Vance said.

"Is that Vance?" Nana asked. "I haven't spoken to him in years."

"Yes, it is," Mike said and handed the phone to his grandmother.

Mike was in awe. By living the superconscious path, his life had completely turned around.

He had a healthy, happy family and had more money than he needed. He had a great marriage, he was on purpose, and was fulfilled with his career. Most of all, he was happy. He went upstairs to play his guitar.

Maybe we'll go on a family vacation, he thought, and smiled before saying aloud, "Magic."

ABOUT THE AUTHOR

Christopher Duncan is the author of the international best-selling book "You're Not Broken". He lives in the Gold Coast, Australia, with his wife, Harriet. He is the founder of The Conscious Education Company which is the premier human transformation company in the world. You can find out more about Chris and his teachings at:

www.christophermduncan.com

Made in the USA
Coppell, TX
14 February 2024

29023526R00125